Perrott Phillips

When in Spain

illustrated by Alex Brychta

J M Dent & Sons Ltd London

Made in Great Britain at the
Aldine Press Letchworth Hertfordshire
for J. M. Dent & Sons Limited
Aldine House Albemarle Street London

This book is set in Times 327, 10 on 11 point.

ISBN 0 460 05894 0

Contents

THE FACE OF SPAIN

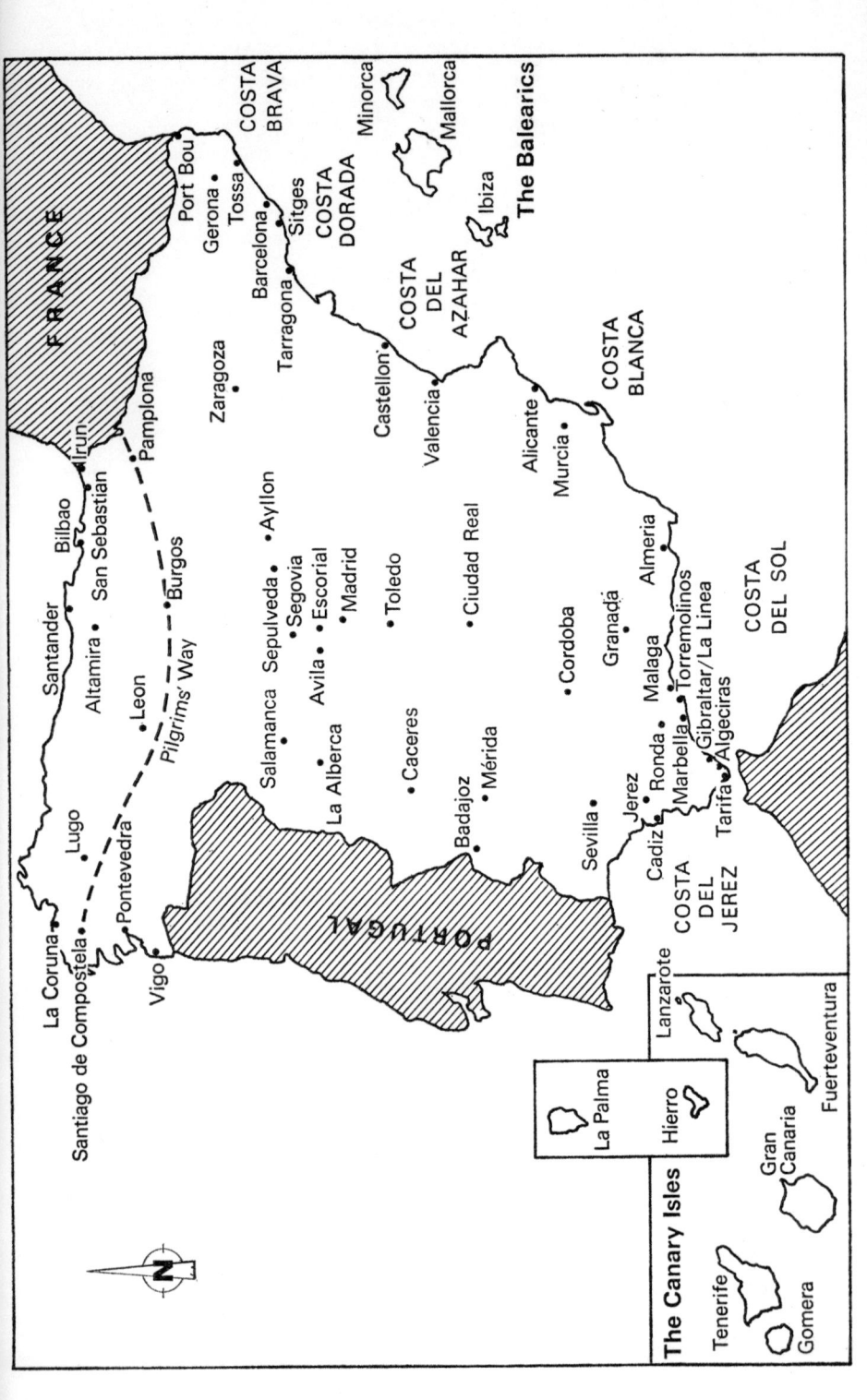

FRANCE

COSTA BRAVA
Port Bou
Gerona
Tossa
Barcelona
Sitges
Tarragona
COSTA DORADA

Minorca
Mallorca
Ibiza
The Balearics

COSTA DEL AZAHAR

Zaragoza

Castellon
Valencia

Alicante
Murcia
COSTA BLANCA

Irun
Pamplona

Bilbao
San Sebastian
Burgos
Pilgrims' Way

Santander
Altamira
Leon

Ayllon
Sepulveda
Segovia
Escorial
Madrid
Salamanca
Avila
Toledo
Ciudad Real

Cordoba
Granada
Almeria
Malaga
Torremolinos
COSTA DEL SOL
Gibraltar/La Linea
Algeciras
Tarifa
Marbella
Ronda

Lugo

La Coruna
Santiago de Compostela
Pontevedra
Vigo

La Alberca
Caceres
Mérida
Badajoz

PORTUGAL

Sevilla
Jerez
Cadiz
COSTA DEL JEREZ

N

The Canary Isles

La Palma
Hierro

Lanzarote
Fuerteventura
Gran Canaria
Tenerife
Gomera

1 So this is Spain

'Tea as Mum Makes It' . . . 'Have a Fistful of British Flavour' . . . 'Chips! Chips! Chips!' . . . 'Bingo Tonite' . . . 'Billy's British Boozer First on the Left' . . . 'We Sell Draught Red Barrel'.

Can this *really* be Spain, you wonder, as the airport bus roars along the southern coastal motorway, past monstrous hotel blocks beached like stranded liners, past festoons of identical souvenir shops, gaudy beer-bars and raucous discos. The answer is yes, at least for a large majority of the three million British holidaymakers who arrive each year and who fondly imagine this kind of concrete *urbanización* represents the real Spain, the proud and tortured birthplace of Goya and El Cid, Cervantes and Queen Isabella, Picasso and Philip II. The sad fact is that most tourists do not end up in Spain at all, but in a strange 'international holiday zone' catering expertly, but hardly typically, for the needs of millions of sunseeking Britons, Germans, French and Scandinavians.

A paradox at the best of times, Spain has excelled herself in becoming the most well-known unknown country in Europe. For the tourist coastline is merely a lace frill fitting uncomfortably round the stern and unchanging face of inland Spain.

After France, Spain is the largest country in Europe, but it is a country which for generations lay asleep under a witch's spell. Away from the bulldozers and the cement-mixers, there are still hidden places where no tourist sandal has disturbed the dust of centuries and the storks still doze in their nests on the church towers.

This is the Spain I love, the Spain we are going to explore and the Spain I hope you will come to love, too.

Spain is not a cosy country and the enrichment you gain from it depends a great deal on your ability to respond to its moods. Some people return vaguely disappointed. They expected to find gipsies dancing flamenco in the streets, bullfighters sitting in the cafés, guitarists strumming at every corner and dark-eyed *señoritas* smiling coquettishly from wrought-iron balconies. 'It wasn't like I thought,' they say. Spain is what you make it and you can journey a long, long way before coming across the cliché-images of the travel posters.

Everyone has his own 'castle in Spain', a private dream of the ideal escapist spot. It need not be a castle; it can be a mountain, a placid lake, a lonely swamp echoing to the call of marsh birds, a treasure-house of a city or a desert as dry as parchment. Spain

can provide all these. What 'total Spain' cannot do is offer a conventional stereotype, present a neatly packaged 'image' or confirm the preconceived ideas of those who visit her with their minds already made up.

Today is yesterday

If I were to choose a word which conveys Spain's most evocative quality, it would be 'timelessness'. In no other place in Europe do you get the feeling, so frequently, that you have suddenly been transported back through the centuries. And it can happen in so many ways. . . .

It is following in the footsteps of El Greco through the cobbled streets of Toledo after dark, and then looking down on the city from the Hermitage of the Virgin of the Valley to see the unchanged landscape he painted at the close of the sixteenth century. It is entering the fortified city of Avila, whose twelfth-century battlements surmount the hill like a crown of gold and which were already venerable when St Teresa was born there in 1515. It is wandering into an old village church, picking up one of the tattered choir books and reading on the title page, 'Office of the Mass. Printed by Montserrat Cancella in Barcelona on February 10, 1686, by favour of His Most Catholic Majesty King Carlos II.' In the capital itself, it is looking up into the small dome of San Antonio de la Florida to find yourself face to face with the smart social set of eighteenth-century Madrid. In 1798, Goya was commissioned to paint a fresco round the inside of the church dome representing the Miracle of St Anthony. He painted an almost three-dimensional balcony, with a fashion-

8

ably dressed throng of people peering over, strolling, chatting and laughing, all with a conspicuous lack of piety. To the acute embarrassment of the church, he also used the faces of prominent court officials and their mistresses. From below, it appears as though they have all come out on the balcony to have a look at you—or at the remains of their unconventional creator. Goya's simple burial place is only a few inches from your feet.

This feeling of timelessness is not confined to the atmosphere evoked by ancient stones or places caught in the powerful time-warp of history. In 'secret Spain' the people themselves possess an almost supernatural ability to conjure up the past, without any effort or affectation.

In the village of La Alberca, near Salamanca, I was stopped in the middle of my evening meal by the sound of a young girl singing in the street outside, her voice floating plaintively on the still air. She was *La Moza de Animas*, a child traditionally chosen by the villagers to wander the streets each evening, ringing a bell and calling for prayers for the dead. It was a sound straight from the Middle Ages.

Along with a party of young people, I once stayed at a pokey inn in the mountain village of Trevelez, above Granada. After dinner, we rigged up an antiquated record-player and danced to the landlord's four records, each one worn as smooth as a soup-plate. Quickly, the word got around that there were exotic foreign girls in town and, one by one, the local Don Juans filtered in, hair sleeked back and looking shorter than ever in their best suits. They lined up against the walls, smiling shyly but hopefully. The more courageous ones danced in a stiff, old-fashioned manner, with perfect decorum, as the capricious electricity supply sent the music whining up and down.

Indeed, it was only a few miles from Trevelez, at Yegen, that a flabbergasted British traveller received a handful of rare Punic and Iberian coins in his change. An old villager had died leaving a hoard of them in a drawer and his sons, not knowing any better, had spent the lot. They had circulated among Yegen's few shopkeepers for years without anyone noticing anything unusual. The coins are now in the Ashmolean Museum, Oxford.

Faced with dreamlike situations like these, you often get the uncomfortable feeling you have somehow fallen through a hole in the twentieth century.

A surprise at the end

There is no easy way of discovering secret Spain and the greatest rewards are often at the end of arduous journeys. On the arid central *meseta* of Old Castile, I once succeeded in driving backwards for three hundred years.

Travelling as the whim took me, I found myself climbing through a wild and mountainous landscape of red clay, past

huddled villages set away from the road, each one as secretive as a clenched fist. Suddenly, a bridge, the pointed arch of a town gate . . . and I was plunged into the seventeenth century. Ox-carts, heavily laden donkeys, women with pitchers of water, farmers in rustic dress carrying heavy staves, aloof horsemen and darting children jostled down the narrow streets to the *Plaza Mayor*. Like a tableau in some over-ambitious historical pageant, the crowd was buying, selling, eating, drinking and gossiping, circulating round the fountain, under the ancient pillared houses and the arcades of the Town Hall and past the curious little church with a house built up against its walls. I had stumbled on market day in the forgotten village of Ayllon and I felt like a visitor from another planet.

No country can live in Yesterday for ever, and Spain's enormous industrial progress is changing the habits and customs of generations. But outside the big towns (and some-times buried deep inside them), old traditions die hard and the sand moves slowly through the hourglass. To understand why this quality of timelessness has been preserved for so long, we must now open the great iron-bound chest that is the history of Spain. . . .

2 The warrior who fell asleep

Now step back 15,000 years

By the light of her candle, little María Sanz de Sautuola saw an astonishing sight. The ceiling of the cave into which she had wandered was covered in paintings of animals, as bright and lifelike as if they had been finished that day. In the flickering light, she recognized bulls, bison and deer. In some of the paintings, the natural contours of the rock had been used to give a startling three-dimensional effect.

María rushed from the cave to tell her father, the archaeologist Marcelino Sanz de Sautuola, who had been excavating the site, just outside the old town of Santillana in northern Spain.

It was with disbelief that Don Marcelino gazed on the paintings, probably the first man to do so for 15,000 years. For not only were they a direct link with the original inhabitants of Spain—a discovery which in itself exceeded his wildest expectations—but they were without question the finest known examples of prehistoric art.

Since that dramatic day in 1875, other cave paintings have been discovered in Spain, but nothing to compare with these red-and-black animals of Altamira, described by one archaeologist as 'The Sistine Chapel of prehistoric art'.

The men who painted them in a mixture of bulls' blood, oil and ochre—and whose creative imagination was thousands of years ahead of its time—lived in the Ice Age and were the first 'Spaniards'.

They didn't live in peace for long. The Iberians arrived from Africa, clashed with Celts moving in from the north and eventually merged to form the dominant Celtiberian tribe. Barely pausing to wipe the blood from their swords, they turned to face the Phoenicians and Greeks—who came as traders and left behind both the vine and the olive—and then the warlike Carthaginians.

Even as early as this, one of the most powerful elements in the Spanish character was already being forged. They were implacable as enemies—brave, stoical, fanatical and with an unnerving capacity for pursuing and wearing down an adversary over the centuries.

The tread of the legions

The native Celtiberians waged a relentless guerilla war against the Carthaginians from what is now Tunisia, who began raiding southern Spain for silver and slaves and finally set up their capital at 'New Carthage' (now Cartagena) in the third century BC.

Spanish freedom-fighters were only the beginning of the Carthaginians' troubles, however. Rome was flexing its muscles in the east and it was only a matter of time before it turned its baleful eye on this new and dangerous area of Carthaginian expansion.

The result was inevitable. By the beginning of the second century B.C., the whole of Spain was shaking beneath the steady and remorseless tread of the Roman Legions. The Carthaginians launched a counter-attack under the brilliant general, Hannibal, who shook the Romans by crossing the Pyrenees and the Alps at the head of an army of men and elephants. But he failed to take Rome, and Carthaginian power was smashed for ever in 146 B.C.

To the long-suffering Celtiberians, the invading Romans were merely the same old enemy in different uniforms. They carried on their stubborn resistance. In 134 B.C., the entire population of Numancia died in the flames of their city rather than fall into Roman hands—one of several examples of mass suicide. Groups of guerillas made lightning attacks on Roman emplacements. Such was Spain's bloodthirsty reputation that some Roman Legions mutinied when told they would have to serve there.

Within a century, the invaders had a firm grip on the country and in the four hundred years that followed, Spain gained far more than it lost from Rome's brand of colonialism. A central administration was formed with Latin as a common language, highways were built, aqueducts were raised and sophisticated sewerage systems undertaken.

With the confidence that only a nation that regards itself as invincible can display, the Romans built for posterity. And their noble and soaring monuments still stir the imagination. In Segovia, the enormous Roman aqueduct strides 900 feet across the main square of the town like the legs of some gigantic column of legionaries. Beneath its 128 granite arches—constructed without cement or water—the townsfolk scurry like ants; cars and buses become mere toys and even the houses which huddle against its feet look like building-bricks left behind by some untidy child.

One searingly hot day, I arrived at the town of Mérida and trudged through the dust to the Roman ruins on the outskirts. The heat struck back from the terraces of the amphitheatre, making the bleached stones almost painful to look at. I descended into the underground dressing-room, which was cool, dark and so ghostly that one could almost hear the excited chatter of the Roman actors as they prepared to go on. Up a few steps to the stage ... and then the light hit me like the blade of a sword and there before me were the rising tiers, just as the

first actor on the stage must have seen them, filled with an expectant audience, eight centuries before the birth of Christ.

The Spanish repaid their debt to their Roman conquerors. The Emperors Trajan and Hadrian were born in Spain, so were the dramatist Seneca, who had the unenviable task of teaching Nero, and the poet Martial. Spanish soldiers, admired by the Romans for their bravery, were recruited to join the freezing legions manning Hadrian's Wall in Britain.

Christianity filtered into Spain through the later Romans—with far-reaching effects—but by A.D. 400 the reach of the Roman Empire had finally exceeded its grasp and the whole structure started to fall apart at the seams.

The seven-hundred-year memory

It was the opportunity the Germanic tribes had been waiting for. First the Vandals poured down through the Pyrenees, laying waste the country as far as Vandalusia (now Andalucia). Hard on their heels came the Visigoths, a much more powerful force who brought with them a tax system, a code of law and the hereditary genes which today result in so many blue-eyed Spaniards.

They also brought something far more momentous. In 589, King Reccared formally pledged himself to the Church of Rome and the banner of Catholicism was raised over Spain.

The Visigoths had a bare three hundred years to enjoy their power, the end of their reign being haunted by the spectre of invasion by the Moors from North Africa.

In 711, the Moors arrived. Hordes of wild Berber tribesmen under the one-eyed Táriq '*El Tuerto*' landed near Gibraltar and hurled themselves into a ferocious war to win Spain for Islam.

Seven years later, the whole of Spain was theirs except for a stubborn pocket of resistance in the north. Notwithstanding the ferocity of their troops, the Arab overlords were cultured men and the Moslem capital of Córdoba became one of the most respected centres of learning in a dark and backward Europe.

Centuries passed but not for a single moment did the Christians in the north forget their vow that, one day, they would drive out the heathen *Moros*. Slowly, their strength increased and in 1063 the long, agonizing crusade of the Reconquest began in earnest.

Brave, fanatical and fired by religious zeal, the Christians fought every inch of the way from their stronghold in León. Aragón and the Castile were the first provinces to be reclaimed and in 1085 Alfonso VI took Toledo.

The Christians had a cunning general—and probably the world's first 'psychological weapon'—in El Cid Campeador (1040–98), a mercenary warrior who fought for the highest bidder. His exploits struck such terror into the Moors that they quaked at the mere mention of his name and even fled from his dead body when it was carried by horse to its last resting place.

Spanish stoicism was tested to its utmost, both in the interminable length of the campaign—occasionally broken by periods of internal strife—and the repeated sacrifices demanded of generations of crusaders. One incident is particularly characteristic. During the siege of Tarifa in 1294, Guzmán the Good learned that the Moors had captured his young son and were holding him hostage. He drew his knife, tossed it from one of the windows in the fortifications and shouted to the attackers, 'You can use it to kill my son, but we will never surrender!' They still point out the window to visitors.

The war of the Reconquest ended in 1492 with the capture of Granada, the last Moorish stronghold. The war had lasted seven hundred years and much of the cruel fanaticism which later disfigured the Roman Catholic Church in Spain can be traced back to the crusaders' belief that they were the only true defenders and interpreters of the faith. Ignored by the rest of Europe, fighting a seemingly endless holy war to reclaim their own land from the infidel, the crusaders gradually began to associate Catholicism with patriotism, to the point where the two ideals became inextricably confused.

In their understandable eagerness to eradicate all memory of the Moors, some misguided Christians committed acts of desecration which would almost have made a Vandal raise his eyebrow. One excess was the building of a full-size Roman Catholic cathedral in the middle of the 850 graceful pillars and arches of the Great Mosque in Cordoba. When King Carlos I, who had carelessly sanctioned the plan, actually set eyes on the monstrous structure in 1526, he burst out: 'If I had known what you were up to, you would not have done it. For what you have made here may be found in many other places, but what you have destroyed is to be found nowhere else in the world!'

The seven-hundred-year war is still so ingrained in the Spanish consciousness that an Englishman who visited a remote mountain village near Granada in 1920 and mentioned that he had fought in the Great War was asked: 'How many Moors did you kill?' To the villager, the Moors had remained the eternal enemy and presumably nobody had told him that they had left Europe in the fifteenth century, never to return.

The wasteland

Meanwhile, in 1474, two of Spain's strongest royal houses had united with the marriage of Isabella of Castile and Ferdinand of Aragón, ushering in an era of unprecedented power and prosperity. Financed by Isabella, Christopher Columbus discovered the New World and the conquistadores colonized Mexico, Florida, Central America, the West Indies, Peru and Chile. The Aztecs of Mexico and Incas of Peru were cruelly persecuted and their awe-inspiring hoards of gold shipped to Spain—only to be squandered on futile military campaigns and the shoring up of a ramshackle new empire in the West.

Spain found itself saddled with a European empire when Carlos I became Charles V, Emperor of the Holy Roman Empire, and inherited the Hapsburg 'properties' of his grandfather in Austria, Germany, Holland, Belgium and Italy.

Difficult to control at the best of times, the colonial situation was made far worse by the appearance of militant religion—this time in the form of the Protestant Reformation, fanning out rapidly and dangerously from Germany.

Charles V found himself spending less and less time in Spain. Tiring of the whole affair, he renounced the Spanish throne in 1556 and retired to the remote monastery at Yuste, where he spent his last years making clocks, eating anchovies, drinking copiously and sitting in his living-room fishing from an artificial lake built beneath his window.

Anti-Protestant purges were continued with increased virulence by his son, Philip II, who made the fatal mistake of trying to claim England for the Catholic faith by sending an Armada in 1588. It was a disaster.

Philip II also ended up in a monastery. For thirty years, he poured untold sums into building the vast and gloomy El Escorial Monastery, the biggest building of its kind after the Vatican and the Kremlin. Built in the shape of a gridiron in memory of St Lawrence—who was supposed to have been roasted alive by the Romans—the Escorial contains 16 patios, 88 fountains, 13 chapels, 9 towers, 15 cloisters, 86 stairways, 1,200 doors and 2,673 windows.

When the people complained that too much was being frittered away on the building, Philip cemented a gold nugget into one of the towers, just to prove there was still plenty of cash left in the coffers. Not that the King lived in any elegance or luxury. As befitted a religious zealot, his own private quarters consisted of a bare, cell-like room. He died there in 1598, after ordering the black drapes for the church and selecting his coffin, made from planks of a galleon that had fought against the Moors.

Philip's death heralded a long and sorry period of depleted finances, inept monarchs and dwindling power. Under the Hapsburgs, Spain reached its lowest ebb. You can see their increasingly prognathous and inbred profiles in the works of successive court painters. Philip III had to send his courtiers round cap-in-hand to supplement his income. Philip IV couldn't have governed a borough council, least of all a great nation, and devoted most of his energies to producing thirty-two illegitimate children. 'Charles the Bewitched' was epileptic and half-witted.

Having driven Spain into bankruptcy, the degenerate Hapsburgs signed the country away to the French Bourbons who succeeded in providing a rather shaky line of monarchs from 1700 until the twentieth century.

During this era, Spain endured every kind of vicissitude, starting with a thirteen-year War of Succession initiated by the Hapsburgs, who felt they had been cheated out of the crown. The Spanish War of Independence—an attempt to shake off French rule—brought the Duke of Wellington and Napoleon Bonaparte tramping across Spanish soil and resulted in the accession to the throne of Ferdinand VII. Unluckily, he turned out to be a despot who gave short shrift to all Spain's liberal aspirations. After a reign marked by persecution, execution and censorship, the last straw came when he ignored the 'no female successor' constitution and bequeathed the crown to his infant daughter, Isabella.

For forty-three years, a series of confused wars was waged to try to get Ferdinand's brother, Don Carlos, onto the throne but in the end Isabella was recognized.

Monarchs came and went, Spain lost her last colonies in South America, toyed with being a republic and ended up in 1923 as a military dictatorship under General Primo de Rivera.

Rip van Winkle awakes

Stagnant, barricaded behind the Pyrenees and immersed in its own problems, Spain had been left centuries behind by commercial, social and economic developments in mainstream Europe.

In 1931, Spain became a republic but a swing to the left at the elections in 1936 raised the bogeyman of Communism and provided an excuse for a right-wing military rising led by General Francisco Franco Bahamonde. Ironically, most of the troops who set sail on his 'Victory Convoy' to reclaim Spain from the infidel Communists were . . . Moorish.

The civil war that followed was conducted with appalling ferocity on both sides, giving full rein to that dark side of the Spanish character that seems to embrace death. In the bloodletting, there was even a strange twist of the hourglass when Guzmán the Good's sacrifice to the Moors was repeated as if 642 years of progress had never taken place.

Besieged within the Nationalist fortress of Toledo, the commander was told on the telephone that the troops of the Workers' Militia had captured his son. Colonel José Moscardo e Iriarte was given ten minutes to surrender the garrison, other-

16   wise his son would be shot.

He was allowed to speak to the boy on the telephone and the poignant conversation that followed is displayed in more than twenty languages in the Colonel's room in the Alcazar, preserved just as it was at that moment:

'Papa!'

'What is happening, son?'

'They say they are going to shoot me if you do not surrender.'

'Then commend your soul to God, shout VIVA ESPANA! and VIVA CRISTO REY! and die like a hero.'

'A very strong kiss, papa.'

'Goodbye, my son, a very strong kiss.'

Shortly afterwards, sixteen-year-old Luis Moscardo was taken out and shot.

Six hundred thousand lives were lost in the war, which ended after three years with General Franco installed as Head of State, Prime Minister and Supreme Military Commander. Shocked and exhausted, Spain fell yet again into the deep sleep of stagnation and it was not until some years after the Second World War that she awoke with a start, like Rip Van Winkle, to find herself in the twentieth century. The first tourists who visited Spain at that time described it as like walking back into the Middle Ages.

Much of the credit for revitalizing Spain must go to the Americans, who began courting General Franco as the 'Cold War' against Russia intensified. In 1953, in exchange for the right to build missile bases in Spain, they allocated millions of dollars in financial aid. The second most important new influence was tourism. With brilliant stage-management, Spain was packaged and projected as a holiday playground and today tourism is her main source of income. The hordes who invade Spain every year now stray no farther than the beaches of the Costa del Sol or Costa Brava.

The next step will be entry into the Common Market, though it has been made clear that there would have to be changes in Spain's political structure first. A president of the EEC has been quoted as looking forward to the day when they could welcome 'a democratized Spain'.

Which is a reasonable enough cue for introducing an unlikely looking figure in a crown and royal robes who has been waiting patiently in the wings. He is the man named by General Franco as his chosen successor. In a surprising reversal of the conventional course of twentieth-century history, Prince Juan Carlos Alfonso Victor María de Bourbon y Bourbon—'Carlitos' to the Spaniards—will become both King and Head of State, thereby wielding more power than a figurehead 'constitutional monarch'.

So once again, Spain will be a monarchy and the crown of Europe's most individualistic and complex nation will descend not only on a Bourbon head . . . but on a man who speaks fluent English and is the great-great-grandson of Queen Victoria.

3 Across the bull's hide

The rain in Spain

Probably the first 'package tourists' to discover Spain were the groups of pilgrims who banded together in the Middle Ages to visit the holy shrine of St James at Santiago de Compostela, in the region of Galicia. One of them was Chaucer's Wife of Bath, who was described in the *Canterbury Tales* as having been to 'Galice at St Jame'. After Jerusalem and Rome, it was the most important place of pilgrimage in the Christian world, with the added advantages of being nearer, cheaper and safer. Thousands of devout British sandals were worn thin on the long trek through France, over the Pass of Roncesvalles and along northern Spain. It wasn't an easy journey, and many fell out before the end. They were often attacked by bandits and were an easy prey for thieves, tricksters, unscrupulous innkeepers and dishonest guides. But there was cheerful company, good food and wine and a bed of sorts at the end of each day. To keep up their spirits, some pilgrims bored holes in their staves so that they could play them like flutes. On they tramped, following the Pilgrim's Way from Pamplona to Logroño, Santo Domingo de la Calzada to Burgos, León to Ponferrada, and finally Villafranca del Bierzo to Santiago itself, with an indulgence from the Pope and a well-earned rest. It is strange to think those place-names were far more familiar to the medieval pilgrim and his friends than to most modern, jet-propelled tourists. The Way of St James is still clearly marked and in Santiago you can buy the identical souvenirs those doughty travellers brought back as proof of their pilgrimage—small, silver scallop-shells, the emblem of the patron Saint of Spain.

'Unknown' northern Spain often comes as a shock to the unwary tourist expecting the rattle of castanets the instant he crosses the frontier at Irún or drives off the ferry at Bilbao. The fertile coastline, buttressed by steep cliffs and rocky outcrops, could easily be mistaken for Scotland. Parallel with the coast, the Cantabrian mountains unfold for 400 miles in a green curtain, rising to 8,600 feet at the Picos de Europa, where deer, wolves and bears dodge the gunsights of Spain's enthusiastic sportsmen.

It is also wet. 'The rain in Spain stays mainly in the plain' may be a reliable way of improving your vowels but it is no use as a reminder to pack your umbrella. Northern Spain is macintosh country for more than its fair share of the year, a fact

which Santiago de Compostela proves conclusively by having an annual average rainfall of 66 inches, 44 inches more than London.

While the tourists gently sauté themselves in suntan oil on the southern beaches, the Spaniards flock to the temperate northern littoral for their own holidays. Desperate to escape from the kiln of Madrid, even the Spanish Civil Service displays a rare turn of speed as it moves, lock, stock and red tape, to the Cantabrian resort of San Sebastián each summer—earning it the nickname of 'Madrid-on-Sea'.

The émigré bureaucrats stand out conspicuously against the local Basques, who are virtually a separate race from the Spaniards, short, thickset, bullet-headed, hearty eaters and devoted to energetic games. They speak their own language, which when written looks strangely like some Aztec dialect, with words like *O'xieto, Idiaquez, Iztueta* and *Azaldegui*.

Bagpipes and porridge

As you move west towards Galicia, the coast turns into a dis-orientated Norway, with deep fjords called *rías* clawing into the rock, a phenomenon which helps the local fishermen to net 28 per cent of the total national catch . . . including those gorgeous fresh sardines, grilled over charcoal in small seafront cafés. To further confuse the visitor, the Galicians have blue eyes and fair hair, play the bagpipes, dance a form of reel and eat something suspiciously like porridge. Here and there, you might spot houses bearing un-Spanish names like 'The Bridge' or 'The Anchorage' and decorated with whitewashed stones arranged to form chains, anchors, badges or other nautical devices. These are the homes of British sea captains who have retired to spend their last watch among old comrades in a landscape reminiscent of their homeland.

Travelling south, you quickly realize that Spain is the most mountainous country in Europe after Switzerland. The area of Spain totals 190,000 square miles, more than twice the size of the British Isles, and much of the mileage appears to be upwards. As if this is not enough, every twist in the road can reveal a complete contrast in scenery. Even now, the white stone cottages which look as though they have been transported bodily from Galway start to slip away, the barns on stilts called *horreos* become fewer, the wooden-shuttered Tyrolean chalets disappear . . . for we are dropping down to the dusty wheatfields of León and the vast plateau of Old Castile.

The glory of the region of León is the golden city of Salamanca, whose Plaza Mayor is probably the noblest in Spain. It took sixty years to build and was completed in 1788—merely the day before yesterday by Salamanca standards. Salamanca is the Oxford of Spain, a lived-in Renaissance monument with palaces, castles, churches and mansions, any one of which would dignify a city twice its size. The *Casa de las Conchas* was built in the fifteenth century, and the deep-gold façade is decorated with magnificent wrought-iron window grilles and studded with sixteen rows of lovingly carved conch shells. In the setting sun, the shells throw long, diagonal shadows on the wall, creating the extraordinary impression that the wall is one enormous, nail-studded door slowly swinging open to reveal . . . who knows what?

At the time *La Casa de las Conchas* was being built, the thirteenth-century University of Salamanca had already reached the height of its influence and was famous throughout Europe for its advanced academic views, While other countries still shrank from such 'heresy', Salamanca was teaching the theories of Copernicus, and Columbus consulted its professors before undertaking his greatest journey.

But Salamanca was not without its trials of conscience. In 1572, Fray Luis of León, the university's most distinguished professor, was betrayed to the Inquisition and jailed on trumped-up charges of teaching heretical theories. He languished in jail for five years before being allowed to return to the work he loved. On his first morning back, a silent and nervous crowd of professors and students watched him mount his dais, waiting for a bitter attack on those who had betrayed him. Fray Luis smiled at the crowd and began, 'As we were saying yesterday . . .' picking up at exactly the point where his lesson had been cut short five years earlier.

Many lesser men have claimed the phrase since, but you can recapture some of the original atmosphere by visiting Fray Luis's classroom in the university, preserved just as it was at that moment of humanity and compassion.

A castle for everyone

If the map of Spain is like a bull's hide stretched out to dry in the sun, then the Guadarrama Mountains form its spinal column, running across the centre in rocky vertebrae and separating the plateaus of Old and New Castile.

Castile rises above sea level to an average height of 2,500 feet and the surrounding mountains have created a natural barrier, preserving its ancient character and customs. The sun beats down on the land like a hammer but, as in north Africa, it gives way to a distinct chill at night—a curse, they say, left by the Arabs on the land they lost.

Here are your 'castles in Spain'. The legend was born in Castile, the home of *castillos*, or fortresses. North of Madrid, they loom up like stone mastiffs every few miles . . . fifteenth-century Cuellar, as white as an iced cake, the flamboyant fortress of Coca, with its towers and turrets clustered together like organ pipes, and Castilnuovo, its Moorish silhouette rising unexpectedly from luxuriant green woodland.

The eagles of the Guadarramas wheel and hover over mountain villages like Sepulveda, which clambers in tiers up a hillside, escaping from the ravine at its heels. Sepulveda's rickety main plaza is dominated by the eccentric Town Hall, whose crumbling façade somehow manages to include a crane's nest, a clock, several towers, a gallery, a wrought-iron balcony, a couple of shops and a massive stone coat of arms.

Through thick pine forests, you reach Turegano, whose church lies in the sturdy embrace of a fifteenth-century castle,

21

its steeple peeping over the top of the battlements as if wondering whether it is safe to venture out. And in Pedraza, the tiny confessional-box plaza in two tiers, supported by honey-coloured pillars, looks just like a theatre set; at any moment you expect a team of stagehands to cart it away.

From the hidden villages of the Guadarramas, you descend to the motorways, underpasses, flyovers, skyscrapers, furious traffic and frantic policemen of Madrid; the central point of Spain, growing uncontrollably like a science-fiction monster, suffocating in summer and freezing in winter. The Madrileños have a phrase for it, ' *Tres meses invierno y nueve meses infierno* ', or, three months of winter and nine months of Hell. As the August sun drums down on a gasping capital, city wits wipe their brows and ask each other, 'Why did Philip II spend all that money on building an imitation gridiron at El Escorial when he could have used Madrid?'

In summer, one of the coolest places in Madrid is the air-conditioned Prado art gallery. The Prado contains treasures that galvanize even the most art-weary tourist . . . Leonardo da Vinci's second version of the Mona Lisa (superior to the one in the Paris Louvre, say the Madrileños), a room full of staggering Goyas, a wonderful self-portrait by Dürer and, for those with strong stomachs, Hieronymus Bosch's terrifying masterpiece *The Garden of Delights*, depicting all the torments of Hell.

One of the most striking pictures in the Prado is Titian's portrait of Carlos V, seated on a horse and wearing a spectacular suit of armour inlaid with gold. No ordinary 'off-the-peg' suit of armour, the Emperor first had a complete mould of himself made in Toledo in 1525. It was taken to Augsburg by the greatest armourer of the age, Koloman Kolmann, who was then able to supply the Emperor with a whole range of superbly fashioned swordproof suitings. You can see the actual suit of armour in the picture in one of Madrid's most fascinating and little-known museums, the Armoury adjoining the Palacio Real. Here are the priceless steel suits worn by the Kings of Spain, not hidden in glass cases but leading huge 'armies' of knights, footmen and magnificently caparisoned horses. To walk into the great hall of the Armoury is to be confronted with a whole medieval battlefield on the march. There is armour not only for monarchs, men and mounts, but even a tiny and rather pathetic suit made for a royal child and an absurd set of armour-plating for a pet dog. If you spot some bullet holes in the armour, don't fall into a trap like one American tourist I overheard. 'See how the invention of firearms ended the whole era of personal armour,' he said eagerly to his companion. 'On the day that bullet hole was made, armour became obsolete.' The truth is far less romantic. Some of the exhibits got in the way of a few stray rounds during the Civil War.

The Madrileños are 'night people', which is why they are nicknamed *gatos*, or cats. I have never ever seen a *gato* yawn,

22

and even the smallest children keep late hours, scampering under the festoons of lights in the Plaza Santa Ana until almost midnight. Students and young people make for one of the oldest and most *típico* streets, the Cava Baja, a short walk down a steep flight of steps from the historic, seventeenth-century *Plaza Mayor*.

The Cava Baja is lined with *tascas*—taverns with low, beamed ceilings and walls blackened with the smoke of centuries, where you can buy a *chato* of wine for twopence—and coaching inns with galleried courtyards and primitive little rooms. At night, the street overflows with local colour, the *tascas* packed with singing crowds, rhythmically clapping hands to a guitar, and the inns filling up with country folk visiting their relatives in the city.

Groups of students called *tunas* and dressed as medieval troubadours go from restaurant to bar to café, serenading the customers. With their pointed black beards, dashing costume and mandolins, they look like figures from a Velazquez painting. One night, I was dining in a beamed and vaulted cellar at one end of the Cava Baja when a *tuna* appeared down the wooden staircase, singing and playing with infectious enthusiasm. They delighted us with traditional songs and dances. And then came a moving moment. As they left, the waiters laid their napkins on the steps under their feet as a tribute to their performance. It was a spontaneous and infinitely touching gesture; gentle proof that in Spain chivalry lives on.

From the Alps to an anvil

West of Madrid, the Guararramas link arms with the Sierra de Gredos range, creating an Alpine fantasy of thickly wooded slopes, cherry orchards, bright-as-a-pin villages and wooden farmhouses reflected in rivers trembling with trout. But before you can fully absorb the scene, the landscapes clash and conflict again like duelling swordsmen. From the emerald richness of the Sierra de Gredos, you find yourself with a bump in Estremadura, the rough, earthy region that jostles the south-western edge of New Castile.

It is a wild land of eagles' nests, vast uncultivated spaces (only 52 million of Spain's 123 million acres are arable), brief wooded areas, dour people and taciturn towns built round ancient manor houses. Estremadura bred the conquistadores who colonized South America—many of the palaces in the venerable hill town of Trujillo were built with their gold—and even now you have to be hardy to toil in this sun-creased terrain where the farmers pray for just a few drops of the rain that falls so generously on the head of St James.

At the eastern end of the Guadarrama 'spine' is the plain of La Mancha, where Don Quixote tilted at the windmills, which rolls almost to the foothills of the Sierra Nevada, the 350-mile mountain wall between us and southern Spain. To get our first glimpse of the Mediterranean, we have to climb to the rooftop of Spain where the endless Sierras winnow away beneath us like a view seen from the window of a plane. Piercing blue gentians pattern the ground like an expensive carpet and the air is heavy with the scent of wild sage. The only sounds are cowbells echoing in the valleys and, if you are lucky, a shepherd boy singing a *copla*, or verse, his reedy voice carried in the thin air until it vanishes like a wraith among the distant peaks.

The Sierra Nevada is one of Spain's main winter-sporting centres and at the right time of year you can ski in the morning and spend the afternoon sunbathing on the Costa del Sol. Soon, we shall be able to dip our toes in the Mediterranean, on the highly developed coastline which stretches from the Costa del Sol through the Costa Dorada and the Costa Brava to the French frontier.

Through the heat-haze to the east is the 'greengrocery' of Spain, the *huertas*, or orchards, citrus groves and market gardens, of Almeria and Alicante. The area is dotted with small villages where stiff-legged, long-beaked storks peer over their nests in church towers, and the cattle in the fields have African egrets perched on their backs like secretaries waiting to take a letter.

Fantasy in Barcelona

The burly, hard-headed region of Catalonia could not come as a greater shock. Industrious and staunchly individualistic, the Catalans have always looked across the Pyrenees to France rather than to the rest of Spain. The commercial capital, Barcelona, has such a determined, businesslike air that it could almost be renamed 'Bustle-ona'. The Catalans are proud of their business sense and regard themselves—to the great irritation of everyone else—as the mainstay of Spain. On the basis that they provide more than their fair share of the national effort, the Catalans frequently mutter about independence, with occasional cries of 'Self-government for Catalonia!'

The Catalans have little time for fantasy or daydreaming, with one startling exception. The most fantastical building in the whole of Christendom stands in Barcelona—the cathedral of La Familia Sagrada, designed by the controversial architect Antonio Gaudí. The four main steeples crane over the city's rooftops like giraffes, but it is not until you reach the building that you realize it is only half finished and open to the skies. It is only too clear why the cathedral roused bitter controversy from the moment the first stone was laid. Its weird, surrealist façade is covered in every kind of decoration. Carved vines writhe up the walls, a flock of stone chickens peck above the main door and the sun glints from pieces of ceramic, crystals and brightly

24

coloured tiles. There is not a straight line in the whole structure, the windows are cave-like holes, the eaves drip and bubble like molten lava and the bottle-shaped spires are tipped by what look like ceramic billiard-balls. The cathedral will probably remain an uncompleted masterpiece, a tantalizing reminder of what might have been. Antonio Gaudí was killed in a street accident in 1925 with the plans forever locked in his head.

Catalonia's other great religious shrine is less controversial but equally dramatic. The Monastery of Montserrat stands 3,900 feet high among a range of jagged, saw-toothed peaks thirty miles behind the city. You can reach it by a hairpin-bent road or by train from the Plaza de Espana, transferring to a cablecar for the last $3\frac{1}{2}$ miles. The setting is incomparable and the ancient legend that Montserrat was 'Monsalvat', the hiding-place of the Holy Grail, inspired Wagner to compose his opera *Parsifal*. The monastery was built in the eighteenth century on the site of a church dating back another 800 years, though religious hermits were living in nearby caves before then. To Spain, Montserrat is sacred as the shrine of *La Virgen Morena*, the Black Virgin, a strange, rather sinister image which is said to have been carved by St Luke. Young Catalan honeymooners traditionally visit the Virgin to ask for her blessing on their marriage. You can stay overnight at the monastery, paying whatever you can afford, and it is an uplifting experience at the end of each day to hear the angelically pure voices of the famous Boys' Choir singing the Catalan hymn, *Virolai . . .*

> *Rose of April, Dark One of the Mountains,*
> *Star of Montserrat*
> *Shed light over Catalonia*
> *lead us up to heaven.*

In the fourteenth century, Pedro IV of Aragon came to ask the Virgin to support his invasion of Majorca. From the peaks above the monastery, reached by funicular, the island is visible on a clear day, a whale-like mass floating far out in the Mediterranean. Now it is invaded by $2\frac{1}{2}$ million tourists each year, with three hundred planeloads a day of them flying in and out of the only airport at the height of the season. But we must turn our back on Catalonia and move south to Andalucia.

The Catalans regard their southern neighbours as backward, workshy and indolent. How irksome it must be for them to stomach the fact that, to the outside world, Andalucia is regarded as 'the *real* Spain'.

Picture postcard province

Imagine for a moment the typical Englishman as pictured by a Spaniard who had only ever seen travel posters. He would be a Morris-dancer in bells, ribbons and straw-hat, dancing to a tambourine and warbling folk-songs about milkmaids and market-day; and in the background would be a thatched cottage. Preposterous? Of course. But no more absurd than the way Andalucia, the least typical of Spanish regions, has come to represent the accepted image of 'Spanish Spain'—complete with castanets, haughty ladies in swirling, polka-dotted dresses, men in flat Cordoba hats, ornate wrought-iron balconies and tiled patios cooled by fountains.

Certainly, Andalucia can reveal aspects of quintessential Spain, but in a way that would completely unnerve the poster-designers. In the Royal Chapel at Granada are the tombs of Spain's greatest monarchs, Ferdinand and Isabella, sculpted in Carrara marble with every kind of noble and florid decoration. The figures—their faces taken from death masks—lie side by side, with Ferdinand's head slightly higher than Isabella's, which has sunk a couple of inches into her pillow. The device was used to suggest masculine superiority but even after death the fanatical and formidable Isabella has the last word; the Spaniards say her head is lower because her brains were heavier. Walking round the tomb one day, I discovered a trap-door and a flight of stone steps leading down to an iron grille. Behind it was the very essence of Spain . . . two leathery coffins with vaulted lids, like large violin-cases, the last resting places of *Los Reyes Catolicos*, Ferdinand and Isabella. Under the pomp and the majesty, just these plain black emblems of the mortality that comes impartially to king and commoner, illuminated by a single, naked light bulb. *That* was the real Spain.

In the sunlight above, the crowds were already piling into their coaches for the drive up the hill to the Alhambra, the great palace conceived as Paradise on earth by the Moors and built between the thirteenth and fourteenth centuries. To the Moors, the most outrageous form of extravagance was to use water purely for pleasure and entertainment. The Alhambra is an essay in inspired ostentation; it seems to float on water. Its intricate wall-carvings, like sheets of lace, are reflected in pools, basins and channels. Water spouts in delicate arcs from behind groves of flowers, runs from the mouths of beasts and pirouettes from hidden fountains. From the guide, we learned that the Arabic script along the walls repeated endlessly the words 'Allah is Conqueror', that the Hand of Fatima over the main entrance represented the five tenets of Islam—Charity, Allah, Prayer, Pilgrimage and Fasting—that the musicians who used to play for the Sultan in the harem were blinded to prevent them seeing the concubines and causing jealousy.

But all the time I could not erase from my mind the memory of those two stark coffins.

It wasn't until I reached Ronda, where Nature has carved out her own awe-inspiring line in sculpture, that my morbid feelings were dispelled. High in the mountains behind the sophisticated resorts of Marbella and Torremolinos, Ronda is a town where the ground has been cut away from under your feet.

Perched on either side of a ravine 900 feet deep, the two halves of the town are linked by a vertiginous little bridge, from which the architect was careless enough to fall to his death in 1761. A short way down the chasm, below the bridge, is a bustling restaurant, balanced on a ledge like a bird's-nest; eccentric, irreconcilable and utterly Spanish, an avowal of life in the face of the two coffins of Granada.

The end of the road

The white mountain villages on the way to Seville, like waste-paper baskets scattered down the hillside, have names like Vejer de la Frontera, Chiclana de la Frontera, Morón de la Frontera. They do not refer to any provincial boundaries but are an echo of the Middle Ages when they marked the dividing line between the lands held by the Moors and the Christians.

In the shadow of Seville Cathedral, the largest in Spain and the biggest Gothic building in the world, I sat in the Courtyard of the Oranges and watched the children playing between the trees. The vermilion fruit shone among the leaves like Christmas-tree decorations. Some boys were sitting on stone slabs playing guitars, a girl clicked her castanets and another put down her satchel and began a sinuous flamenco dance. A gipsy woman came up to me, put her fingers to her mouth in a gesture of eating and asked for alms, '*Una limosnita por amor de Dios*'. It is the anachronisms, sometimes harsh and alarming, that make Spain so fascinating. Here in this cathedral, where fifty masses are said to a Christian God each day, the bell rings from a Moorish tower called the Giralda. Inside, man has created some of the most life-enhancing works of art, yet near by, at the sixteenth-century hospital of La Caridad, hangs a painting of human putrefaction so nauseating that the artist Murillo said one had to hold one's nose when looking at it. The painting was commissioned from the artist Valdés-Leal by Don Miguel de Manara, who renounced a licentious and selfish life to join the brothers of La Caridad after seeing a corpse pass by bearing his own face. Don Miguel had a lot to repent about, for he was said to be the original Don Juan. An anachronism indeed; but then, even the Spaniards themselves refer to their country as 'The Land of the Unexpected'.

And now we have run out of land. If you carry on through Andalucia as far south as you can without falling off the edge, you come to Tarifa, an uncompromisingly Moorish town founded by the Arabs in 711 and immured behind ochre walls. It is a long way in every sense from the green hills of Galicia and when you gaze out from the ramparts, you realize exactly why a perplexed Napoleon said, 'Europe ends at the Pyrenees'. For here you are barely eight miles from Africa.

4 Inside the Spaniard

The rose and the thorn

The most poetic gesture of the annual Poets' Competition, held in the Plaza del Rey in Barcelona, is reserved for the final, prize-winning ceremony. The author of the third best poem receives a rose made of silver. The second prizewinner is presented with a rose of pure gold. The first prizewinner is handed a perfect natural bloom.

It is an elegant demonstration of *gracia*, the much admired Spanish quality of style, grace and warmth. If the rose represents *gracia*, however, then its thorns are probably more typical of certain other Spanish characteristics. 'There is a scarcity of water and an excess of fire in the Spanish temperament', wrote the philosopher Salvador de Madariaga, and although he was referring to the excesses of the Civil War, he could have been commenting on those two prickly virtues so dear to the Spanish soul, *duende* and *pundonor*.

In common with all the most interesting words, *duende* is virtually untranslatable. In searching for a definition, one starts with 'panache', works through 'taste' and 'dignity', ends up with 'inspiration', tries combining them all and still fails to pierce its core. One thing is certain: whatever *duende* is, it cannot be contrived. *Duende* is something which happens to a person, or wells up from his innermost being. A great orator stirring the emotions of an audience to its very depths achieves *duende*. A flamenco-singer, possessed by a cadence which seems to defy all laws of respiration, has *duende*. A bullfighter whose style and courage are fused in a moment of inspiration demonstrates quintessential *duende*. A building of dignity and charm can reflect *duende*, even a stage play where every element is perfectly balanced produces a corporate *duende*.

The word is by no means archaic. You hear it in Spain every day and it is the highest compliment you can pay. Sometimes it is used affectionately. I once saw a little English boy trip over while running to buy an ice-cream. He badly grazed his knee and his handful of *pesetas* went flying. Forcing back his tears, he doggedly gathered the coins together, bought his ice-cream and returned to his parents with a brave smile. 'What *duende*!', chorused all the Spanish mothers.

As profound as *duende* is *pundonor*, the rigid Spanish concept of pride and honour. Appearances count for everything in Spain. The girl you see in the evening *paseo*, dressed in a smart

new outfit, probably packs it away in tissue paper the moment she gets home. It is the only one she has. That neat young man in a dark suit and shiny shoes has to take two jobs, one in the daytime and one at night, to keep his head above water. That group sitting all afternoon round a café table, apparently at leisure, are using it as their 'business premises' because they can't afford office space. The old servant taking the children for a walk has left a house where her employers are worrying where the next *peseta* is coming from. All of them are bound together in the Spanish determination to keep up a dignified front, whatever the odds.

The worst disaster that can befall a Spaniard is to be stripped of his pride and dignity, and the Spanish have such a terror of losing face that one writer described them, most perceptively, as 'the Japanese of Europe'.

The quickest way to invite contempt is to appear drunk in public. It is regarded as an unpardonable social sin. Even after years of mass tourism, Spaniards are disgusted at the sight of drunken tourists lurching back to their hotels. One Spanish friend of mine, who has lived in London for five years, is still shocked when British acquaintances tell him, 'We had a wonderful time last night. We got *so* drunk . . .'

The rather self-conscious *pundonor* of some Spaniards has its funny side, as anyone who has read *Don Quixote* knows. In certain upper-class Spanish circles, it is a matter of social status to have a pale complexion. Girls rarely venture out of doors and babies have their prams shaded with frilly canopies. 'Only peasants working in the fields are suntanned', was the haughty explanation I was given.

In a population of more than 32 million, where it is estimated that 90 per cent of the nation's wealth is in the hands of 10 per cent of the population, the proportion of 'have nots' far exceeds the 'haves'. The constant struggle which constitutes everyday life in poor areas has bred a sardonic humour where Death gets the last and biggest laugh. 'Black' jokes abound in Spain. A friend once referred to the coffin—nicknamed *La Guitarra*, 'the guitar'—as 'the final package-tour', a typically morbid quip.

Like a churchyard full of tombstone inscriptions, the Spanish language is rich in lugubrious proverbs illustrating the inevitability of death. *La vida es un soplo* ('Life is but a puff of air'), *Venimos emprestados* ('Our lives are only loaned to us') and *La muerte no para* ('Death stops for no one') are among the more cheerful. Small wonder that V. S. Pritchett wrote in *The Spanish Temper*, 'Sombreness is so much the dominant aspect of these people that one is puzzled to know how the notion of a romantic and coloured Spain has come about.'

As in Britain in the Middle Ages, superstition always goes hand in hand with 'gallows humour'. I made the mistake of asking a Spanish friend in a bar, '*Le gustaria una última bebida?*' ('Would you like a last drink?'). His eyes rolled and he gripped the counter as if I had cast the Evil Eye upon him. '*No diga nunca una última bebida,*' he croaked, '*siempre una penúltima bebida*'. ('Never say the last drink, always the last-but-one.') For the same reason, the Spanish are reluctant to book theatre or bullfight tickets weeks in advance. It is tempting providence.

Kind hearts and cockfights

The Spanish preoccupation with death, which reaches its climax in the ritual of the bullfight, has led many people to accuse them of an indifference to suffering. On this point, it is worth remembering that the two most savage indictments of war ever painted were both by Spanish artists, Goya's *Mayo 3, 1808* (you can see it in the Prado Gallery in Madrid) and *Guérnica*, by Picasso. The Spanish can certainly be incomprehensibly cruel, as a visit to any cockfight will prove. The sport was banned in Britain as long ago as 1849, but you will find cockpits even in Madrid, full of flying feathers and the shouts of punters.

As the Spanish never tire of telling you, however, there is no need for a Society for the Prevention of Cruelty to Children. The sentimental, and often hypocritical, love of animals we profess in Britain is really more the product of a high standard of living than any conscious attempt to emulate St Francis.

In Spain, all the love we dissipate on animals is channelled to the children, who are spoiled, fussed and doted over to a degree which would horrify the average British nannie. It is almost a point of national policy. When the formation of a society for the prevention of cruelty to animals was suggested, the organizers were criticized by the Roman Catholic press as 'old maids who have become perverted because they have failed to bear children', and the association eventually devoted itself to 'the protection of animals and plants'. Church officials in one town also

gave the thumbs down to a showing of Walt Disney's animal film *Bambi*, on the grounds that it tended to divert human sympathy, and thereby individual charity, away from the relief of 'those made in God's image'.

A family affair

Although family ties in Spain are still strong, home life is no longer the prison it used to be for young people. The last ten years have seen a social revolution caused not only by higher prosperity but by the progressive attitudes introduced by mass tourism. A few years ago, mini-skirts were unknown, a girl in trousers caused 'tut-tutting' in the streets, and the idea of a boy and a girl going out by themselves was unthinkable. Huge and daunting *dueñas*, or chaperones, accompanied girls to dances or social functions and marriages were frequently arranged between families. The nearest a boy and girl got to meeting casually would be a shy exchange of glances as they passed in the formal evening *paseo*, or stroll, men on one side of the street and women on the other. Engaged couples would behave with the strictest decorum, hardly daring to hold hands in public, and courtship was often conducted in a highly stylized fashion, with a series of set 'speeches' in ascending order of passion, delivered by the suitor over a period of months. The instant a girl married, she wore black.

Although pockets of resistance still fight on in rural areas, all this has changed. Young people in Spain may behave in a way which appears old-fashioned by our not necessarily superior standards, but they are enjoying their new-found freedom in a manner which would have had their parents denounced from the pulpit.

One little echo of the past remains—the private investigation by parents of a prospective son-in-law's 'suitability'. Spanish newspapers are full of advertisements by private detectives offering '*Investigaciones reservadísimas prematrimoniales*'. If you have your eye on a beautiful Spanish girl, that man on the corner with dark glasses may well have his eye on you.

As there is no divorce in Catholic Spain, this pre-marital caution is logical. The reason why so many Spanish wives run to fat is said to be that they have no fear of ever losing their husbands! All the same, women have long been regarded as an inferior class and emancipation has been a slow process. Women are, however, treated with the greatest courtesy and Spanish manners tend to make the offhand British attitude to women appear almost oafish.

Spanish language is flowery at the best of times. *A sus pies, señora!* ('At your feet, madam!') is an everyday compliment, and although entertaining at home is far rarer in Spain than here, when you leave a friend's house he will say expansively, '*Ha tomado usted posesión de su casa.*' ('You have taken possession of your home.') or '*Ya sabe usted donde tiene su casa.*' ('Now you know where your home is.')

A whisper in your ear

Since every Spanish girl is brought up to believe she is *guapa*, or pretty, a compliment to a girl's beauty is invariably embroidered in the most ornate language, finding its fullest expression in the *piropo*. This is the whispered tribute ardent Spaniards make in the street to passing beauties.

Technically forbidden since 1926—when a *piropeador* was shot by a furious husband—the *piropo* is often formal and poetic, sometimes risqué, frequently suggestive but always basically harmless. Among the more printable are 'If you dived into the Arctic Ocean, the water would boil!', 'When you were born, a piece of heaven fell' and 'Where did you get those almonds you have for feet?'

If you hear a *piropo* hissing towards you in a Spanish street, never stop, smile or answer back. The unwritten rule is to carry on with head held high in such a way that it is clear you have heard the compliment, appreciate it, but have no intention of responding. Never acknowledge the *piropeador* by looking at him. It will give him altogether the wrong ideas—and, for all you know, the *piropo* might have been a naughty one.

Centuries ago, in Seville, it used to be the custom for the courtiers to drink the water in which the ladies of the court had bathed. When Pedro the Cruel reproached one of his knights for not complying with the custom, he replied, 'Sire, I should fear lest having tasted the sauce, I should covet the bird.' The bathwater tradition has long been thrown out, but such romantic gallantries live on in the *piropo*.

In Spain, the singers may change but never the song.

5 The most brutal ballet. The great Flamenco mystery

Don't boo the bullfighter

If you had elbowed your way through every bullfight crowd in Spain, you couldn't have found a more contrasting couple than the two British tourists who took their seats on either side of me at the *Plaza de Toros* in Seville. It was plainly their first bull-fight but their reactions were entirely different.

The first one, a woman aged about thirty-five, left, white-faced, after ten minutes, pausing only to shout a most unlady-like word at the matador in the arena. The second, a young man in his early twenties, sat tight and tried to outdo the local *aficionados*. He bellowed *Olé!* non-stop, irrespective of what was happening in the ring, squirted wine from a wineskin into his mouth with the thirst-crazed passion of a rescued castaway, booed in the wrong places and shouted to the arena president to award two ears to one of the matadors who had given a quite workaday performance.

Of course, both attitudes were equally misguided. If the thought of killing bulls sickens you, then my advice is simple: Do not go at all. The part of the bullfight every British tourist loves—the colourful procession into the arena which starts the afternoon—lasts only a few minutes. After that, rightly or wrongly, you must resign yourself to seeing blood, for that is what it is all about. You impress nobody and achieve nothing by stalking out. After all, would you go to an opera, listen to the overture and then leave angrily because you didn't like singing?

On the other hand, it is equally absurd to try to be an instant *aficionado*, or bullfight expert. Nothing irritates the Spanish more than tourists who dress up like bit-players in *Carmen* and then proceed to mimic and trivialize the emotions of the bull-ring. Imagine a Spaniard in a bowler pretending to be an Englishman and shouting ill-informed comments at a cricket match and you will have some idea of the effect.

It is not the right place here to enter into a debate on whether bullfighting is deplorable or not (anyway, by now you have probably sensed where my sympathies lie), but if you do go to a *corrida* then it is better to know something about what the Spanish call *La Fiesta Brava*, and why it appeals so profoundly to the national character. To understand the bullfight is to understand the Spanish.

The one who has to die

For a start, bullfighting is not a sport, as nobody can 'win' in the conventional sense.

It is a combination of ritual sacrifice and disciplined ballet, coupled with an exhibition of skill and bravery, presented in the form of a traditional spectacle. Basically a primitive tableau of man pitted against the forces of nature, it appeals to a fatalistic part of the Spanish character and it displays two of the qualities most highly regarded in a Spaniard . . . arrogance and courage. More than anywhere else, it is in the crucible of the bullring that the Spaniard hopes the divine spark of *duende* will be struck.

The bullfight season lasts from March to October and the traditional day is Sunday, although Madrid also has Thursday bullfights and there are always extra programmes during fiestas — particularly in Seville during Easter.

If you go to a bullfight, try to make sure it features one or two of the most famous matadors. Beware of *novilladas*—bullfights where beginners show their skill, or lack of it—and keep well clear of phoney displays in miniature bullrings organized purely as a tourist attraction. A sad sign of lowering standards in the 'pop' resorts is the mock-bullfight where tourists in braces and baggy flannels are encouraged to make passes at baby bulls, and vendors sell bullfight posters with your own name printed among the list of matadors. This dreadful charade is usually included as part of a coach excursion and contains more embarrassment to the square inch than anything else I know.

Unlike most things in Spain, bullfights begin promptly, usually at about 5.30 in the afternoon. Always arrive in good time as the entrances are invariably jammed with people, and buses and taxis take ages to hoot through the crowded streets. It is wise to book in advance, either from your hotel porter or from one of the ticket kiosks or *taquilas* in the town. These can be elusive, however, and have eccentric opening times. If you are staying just outside town, the most sensible idea is to buy your ticket from a travel agent who will include the return coach fare in the price.

If the worst comes to the worst, you can always buy tickets at the bullring *taquila* right up until a few minutes before the start, but the clerk is unlikely to speak English and there will be an impatient crowd pressing behind you.

There are two distinct categories of seating in the *Plaza*: *Sol*, where the sun will beat down on your head for most of the afternoon, and *Sombra*, which means you will be in the shade. Sometimes there is a third alternative, *Sol y Sombra*, where you will be roasted for only half the performance until the lengthening shadow of the arena moves your way.

The *Sombra* seats are the most expensive, but whatever the position of sun or shade, the dearest places are those nearest the ringside, the *barreras*. The higher you go, the cheaper you get;

which is why the noisiest section of a bullfight audience can be found in the topmost gallery in the sun.

A star on four legs

Every bullfight conforms to a preordained pattern, beginning with the spectacular procession into the ring of the three matadors followed by their *cuadrillas* or teams of assistants, and various uniformed officials.

Usually, six bulls are killed in an afternoon. The senior matador kills the first and fourth bulls, the second kills the second and fifth and the third man takes the third and sixth. These bulls are not farmyard animals. They are specially bred to fight and kill. None of them has seen a bullfighter before and none will ever see one again.

The star of the bullfight is, in fact, the bull and it is he who controls the pattern of the spectacle. The fiercest breed of fighting bull is the Miura, but you are unlikely to see one in action as most bullfighters refuse to confront them.

When the door of the stockade flies open and the first bull charges into the arena, one of the assistants will trail his cape at him and probably dart behind one of the protective barricades which line the perimeter. You must stifle your impulse to shout 'Coward!' He is merely testing the reactions of the bull, studying the way it moves, what part of the ring it prefers, which horn it hooks with, how accurate is its vision.

The matador depends on his assistants to reveal these qualities. If the matador assesses them correctly, he may give a great display. If he doesn't, he may end up in the *enfermería*. The preliminaries over, the matador himself displays his own skill with the heavy, ceremonial cape. Matador means 'One who kills' and although every matador is also a *torero*, very few *toreros* are matadors.

Every pass with the cape has a name and the matador usually begins with a series of *verónicas*, with the cape spread wide, swinging it past the body, almost pulling the bull's snout with it. This can be repeated several times, with variations, until it looks as though the bull's nose is glued to the cape and the matador has gained complete mastery. But it is just the beginning.

Look down in anger

Now comes the moment most British tourists loathe . . . the appearance of the mounted *picadors* with their long, sharp lances. Let me make one thing clear: they are not there just to torture the bull or to weaken it for the matador. The proud hump of flesh on top of the bull's neck is its tossing muscle. Until the power of that muscle is reduced, the bull will not keep its head down and it cannot be killed by the matador's sword. For the area on a bull's neck—no bigger than a 50p piece— which leads directly to its heart will not be exposed unless it has

35

its front feet together and its head lowered. The lethal power of the bull is in no way reduced, as many a dead bullfighter has proved.

It is the picador's job to attack the muscle with his lance, often meeting the bull's charge head-on, bracing his legs against the flanks of his horse, turning on the lance, pushing until his muscles bulge under his sleeves . . . and the British spectators howl with fury. Often the bull attacks the horse, which is heavily padded with what look like old mattresses, and lifts it clear of the ground, picador and all. This again helps to tire his neck muscles.

Whenever the battle between bull and picador gets too aggressive, the matador, often helped by the other two matadors on the bill, intervenes and lures the bull away with his cape. With any luck, you will see some exciting capework as the matador demonstrates his skill to his rivals.

After this comes the placing of the *banderillas*, sharp, decorated darts which are plunged pair by pair into the bull's shoulders. This can be done by one of the matador's assistants, but it is becoming more common for the matador to place the *banderillas* himself.

The final scene of the spectacle is the *faena*. First the playing of the bull with a tiny scarlet flannel cape called a *muleta*, which replaces the large dress cape. And then the kill.

The last act

The Spanish call the kill '*La Hora de Verdad*', the moment of truth. For it is at this climactic point that the risk to the matador is sharpest, and the moment of truth could well be his last.

Before the matador embarks on the last act, he will dedicate the bull to the bullring president, to a distinguished guest in the audience or to a girl-friend. If he holds his *montera* hat above his head and turns slowly round to acknowledge the whole

36

audience, it means he is dedicating the bull to the crowd. It is a moment to remember, the prelude to a scene of almost unbearable tension.

As the bullfighter plays the bull with his *muleta*, the battle of life and death seems reduced to its most simple and fundamental proportions. Again and again, the matador 'flags' the bull with the *muleta*, turning it so close to his body that the blood from the animal spreads over his *traje de luces*, the 'suit of lights'.

Now it is time for the moment of truth. Slowly, squaring the bull into the head-on position with forefeet together, the matador slides his sword from behind the *muleta*, braces himself and then hurls himself between the horns, his *muleta* sweeping over the bull's eyes, bringing its head down, his sword plunging through the fatal spot into the heart. Deftly, the matador clears the horns and lets the bull sag glassy-eyed to the sand. Unless he is unlucky. . . .

For a stylish performance—and often encouraged by handkerchief-waving from the crowd—the president of the bullring has the right to award the matador trophies from the dead bull, ranging from an ear for a good display to both ears and the tail for an outstanding performance. Maybe, on your first bullfight, you will see an exhibition of great skill and bravery, possibly even be present at the award of two ears. More likely, you will be bitterly disappointed at a spectacle of near-butchery relieved only by sporadic moments of grace and courage. Bulls and matadors are unpredictable creatures and, as in any other art form, inspiration is something that can never be guaranteed. But when you see it, you will know it.

Bullfighters are the highest-paid men in Spain. The flamboyant El Cordobés earned £9,000 for each appearance and by the time he was thirty-five, in 1971, he had a personal fortune of £12 million, several farms, two factories, an hotel, a castle, a private plane, two Rolls-Royces, a yellow Jaguar and a fleet of Mercedes.

But before you criticize them too severely for the part they play in this admittedly barbaric spectacle, remember they rarely retire. Many bullfighters die with their suit of lights on and the screams of the crowd in their ears. More than 280 matadors have died this century. The greatest of them all, Manolete, was fatally gored when he turned his disdainful back on a bull he thought he had killed.

As the Spaniards say: 'The matadors only borrow their money from the bulls. In the end, the bulls always take it back.'

Maybe that is the real truth behind *La Hora de Verdad*.

THE GREAT FLAMENCO MYSTERY

There must be a word for it

A guitar throbs into life, the heels of the dancer beat a rapid tattoo on the wooden floor, the castanets click and rattle and a singer begins a long, wailing, passionate chant. . . .

This is flamenco, the hypnotic, Moorish-sounding folk music which many people regard as 'typically Spanish'. Yet you can travel across three-quarters of the country without ever hearing a guitar twanged or a foot stamped. The Galicians have their *muneira*, they dance the *giraldilla* in León, prefer the *fandango* in Almeria, stick to the *jota* in Aragon and stay loyal to the *sardana* in Catalonia.

The south is the place for flamenco. You can hear it in cafés and bars, in gipsy caves and elegant night clubs. You listen with hundreds of others at an open-air fiesta or discreetly hire your own group for a private performance.

Like bullfighting, flamenco is inextricably woven into the pattern of Spanish life, yet one important strand is missing. Flamenco is one of Spain's great mysteries. Over many years, folklore experts have tried to trace flamenco music back to its exact and original sources, but without success. They even disagree over the origin of the name.

There have been some ingenious theories. One suggestion was that the music was brought to Spain centuries ago by Flemish gipsies, another that it was introduced by Arab immigrants called *fellah-menkus*. A further body of experts hold that flamenco means 'flamingo' and describes the appearance of the dancers, with their slim waists and long legs. Their claims are countered by researchers who insist that the word means 'flamboyant', referring to the exuberance of the performers. While the experts argue about its origin, however, the Spanish are content just to enjoy the music.

Flamenco falls into two main groups, *cante chico*, which consists of fairly light songs with their accompaniments, and *cante jondo*, which is quite the opposite, sombre, passionate and intense.

It is the *cante jondo* or 'deep song' which sounds most strange to British ears. A critic has said of the songs: 'They are not meant for puny creatures or weak stomachs. To an inattentive or superficial ear they may even appear monotonous—so does the long tale of the world's suffering.'

Cante jondo is the ideal vehicle for expressing anguish, a feeling dear to the Spanish heart. In the old days, when every southern town had its flamenco café, the listeners were often more interested in watching the singer suffering than hearing his singing. Nothing pleased them more than when the singer wove his own personal sorrows into the verses, referring to his disappointments, failures, agonies and unhappy love affairs.

The growing popularity of the lighter style of flamenco has tended to soften the harsher edges of the art. These days, you will probably hear only *cante chico* in the nightclubs and cafés.

Each type of flamenco rhythm has its own name and so do the actions of the singers and dancers. The distinctive dry hand-clapping is called *palmada*, the foot-stamping is *zapateado* and the sinuous clicking of the fingers is known as *pito*. It is said that only a Spanish gipsy can really clap in perfect rhythm, so it is not surprising that the most irritating thing an ordinary listener can do is to start clapping in time to a flamenco performance, or worse still, out of time. I once saw a group of over-enthusiastic tourists completely wreck a show with their unsynchronized clapping. The performers were so confused they couldn't carry on.

The most thrilling flamenco can be heard in Seville during Holy Week each April, when groups and even individuals perform in the open with a fervour and authenticity that no nightclub or stage performance could ever capture. In fact, any fiesta in the southern province of Andalucia—the cradle of flamenco —will feature performances by local groups. Some towns (like Córdoba, Sanlúcar de Mayor, Cabra, Vélez Málaga and Tarifa) have annual flamenco contests where groups compete against each other.

The city of Granada has almost made a tourist industry out of its gipsy flamenco dancers, who live in rather luxurious caves in the side of the Sacromonte mountain. The time to go is after dark (preferably with a guide) when the gipsies will leap into action the instant your hand hovers anywhere near your wallet.

If you have the money, you can also hire your own *cuadro flamenco* group for an evening, sit them in a corner of a café and invite all your friends in for a command performance.

Nothing is worse than amateur, leaden-footed flamenco and the standard of performance at many 'touristy' hotels and nightclubs can vary from disinterested to disgraceful, with the added horror of 'audience participation'. The sight of an elderly American matron being encouraged to stamp around the stage with a rose between her teeth has to be seen to be disbelieved.

But there can still be surprises. I remember seeing an extremely fiery and convincing dancer who completely stole the show in a popular Costa del Sol night club. She turned out to be a girl from Cheshire who had run away and married a Spanish guitarist.

THE FACTS OF SPAIN

6 Getting out and around

By plane

One of the oddest sights in Spain is to see crowds of peasants in straw sandals, complete with mountainous luggage, boxes of fruit and live chickens strung together by their legs, waiting at an airport to catch a plane to a provincial town. It is worth taking their tip and tagging along behind with your rucksack.

If the thought of long, hot and tiring overland journeys makes you wilt—and no country seems to pack in more land to the square yard than Spain—you can rise comfortably above it all by using the regular AVIACO 'flying taxi' services which link most major Spanish cities.

Nor will you crash through your holiday budget. Bilbao to Madrid works out at about £13 and Madrid to Malaga approximately £14.80, which means that for £27.80 you can cross the entire country in a matter of hours instead of days and arrive as fresh as a mountain daisy in southern Andalucia.*

By train

They say only two things start on time in Spain: the Talgo and the Toros. *Los Toros* is the bullfight, which always begins 'on the dot' with a bugle call. The Talgo is a high-speed express train which starts equally punctually at the sound of the railwayman's whistle. All other times in Spain should be regarded as '*o asi*' or 'thereabouts'. Modern and luxurious, the Talgo service covers most major cities and is the pride of RENFE, the Spanish national rail system. But it is the most expensive form of rail transport, followed by the TAF and TER diesel and electric services.

With one eye on your pesetas, it's best to stick to the ordinary rail network, which will cost you about 2p a mile 1st Class and half that if you move down to the 2nd Class. It is a painful memory, but there used to be a regular 3rd Class category, which has now almost disappeared. Few people are desperate enough to use it, but as a form of interminable torture it would have delighted the Spanish Inquisition. If your money is running low, don't seek out the last remaining third class carriages but invest in a *kilométrico*, which cuts your rail fares by 20 per cent, provided you travel more than 3,000 kilometres. It entitles you to any number of journeys and is a superb moneysaver if you intend to stick to the rails.

* All prices quoted correct at time of going to press.

By coach and bus

With mountain ranges separating many areas of Spain, distances can be deceptive and what looks on the map like a simple little journey can well grind on for hours—mostly uphill and round unnerving hairpin bends.

Spanish long-distance coaches are excellent and cost around 1p a mile, sometimes with a cheaper fare if you are content to sit in the back. It is essential to book your seat in advance.

But small places still have to rely on local buses, often ramshackle vehicles which leave early in the morning and don't reappear again until well after dark.

It is the cheapest form of travel, but you must be prepared for any kind of vehicle, from some antiquated bone-shaker with wooden seats to a more modern affair with automatic doors.

In some sliding-door varieties, like the buses which run from the frontier town of Irun to the popular resort of San Sebastian, you must enter through the door nearest the driver. The only time I ever saw a Spaniard behave thoroughly unpleasantly to a foreigner was when a tourist hopped in at the back, forced his way through the passengers and then tried to pay the driver while the bus was moving. On the Costa del Sol, however, you get in at the back and pay the conductor before taking your seat.

On all stop-and-carry-one services, the bus-stop is marked *Parada*, although on some country roads the spot is a matter of tradition rather than recognition, the actual sign having been swept away years before by some thundering *camion*. If in doubt, keep your eye open for knots of people standing about and looking hopefully up the road.

Spaniards have all the time in the world, except when they get behind the wheel of a vehicle and are gripped by a demoniac

urge for speed. To stop a bus anywhere, you must signal plainly with your hand, preferably the moment the bus appears as a speck in the distance. Save your time if the sign *Completo* is propped up on the windscreen. It means 'Full up', and the bus won't stop.

By taxi

This isn't as silly as it seems. Spain is one of the few countries in the world where you can take a taxi without clutching the seat in front and watching the figures on the meter shooting up like a demented adding-machine. If you're travelling with friends, it can be cheaper than crossing a city by bus. There is a standing charge of 10 pesetas and the meter adds 5 pesetas a kilometre. The sign *Libre* means the cab is free and the roughly scrawled word *Descanso* or *Almuerzo* on a piece of cardboard means the driver doesn't intend to interrupt his siesta for anyone.

The only taxis to avoid are the ones marked *Gran Turismo*. They have no meter and no green light, and they charge a minimum of 150 pesetas. They are useful for long journeys, but disastrous for nipping into town. The driver won't warn you and it is useless arguing the toss with him at your destination.

By thumb

Hitch-hiking has never really caught on in Spain and the unmistakably disapproving official attitude is that it is 'not illegal, but not encouraged'. There is no word in Spanish for hitch-hiking and 'thumbing' is soberly referred to as *mandar hacer alto a un coche*. All of which doesn't inspire any great confidence as you stand there on the N3 from Madrid to Valencia with the fruit lorries flashing past.

You'll get farther with less effort on the inland roads—particularly across the great central *meseta*, or plain—but thumbing becomes hard work once you hit the coast. In the north, drivers are only concerned with getting a few kilometres under their fanbelt before the next *corniche*, and in the south you'll be caught in a furious two-way traffic between the popular resorts and the North African ferry-port of Algeciras. As one student put it: 'Hitchhiking on the southern coast road is like taking part in a charity walk at Le Mans.'

Spanish drivers still regard hitch-hiking girls as an extraordinary novelty and will slow down, stare, grin toothily and then drive on.

Once in the car, however, you must expect to bat along at a hair-raising pace, as most Spaniards seem to regard driving as an extension of bullfighting. At least you'll have no trouble with tiresome advances, unplanned diversions and sudden shortages of petrol. The type of Spaniard who drives a car is likely to preserve the most punctilious attitude to women. Two girls I met told me how one driver stopped after a few miles and, smiling wolfishly, reached into his pocket for a bundle of photographs. 'Oh dear!' they thought, fearing the worst. The pictures opened out into a concertina and showed his five children—all girls—and his wife. With touching pride, he said: 'And she is the most beautiful girl of them all.'

Hitch-hiking isn't just a matter of standing at the roadside and flagging down any passing vehicle. You can get a head start by looking reasonably presentable. Long hair doesn't matter too much but the Spanish, who are quite obsessively neat themselves, abhor scruffiness. Be selective about your routes, too, going the long way round if the road is more picturesque. There's no problem pinpointing the scenic routes—they are marked in green on the excellent Michelin and Firestone maps.

STAYING PUT

Hotels

When you arrive at a hotel, look at the back of your bedroom door or your wardrobe. You'll find an official notice, impressively rubber-stamped, which gives you the exact price of your room in both high and low seasons and the rates for all meals. If you have been charged more, then your hotelier is in for a nasty encounter with the local magistrates, for nearly all accommodation in Spain is strictly controlled by the government. Once they are fixed by the official grading system, rates cannot be raised except on special and clearly defined occasions, like an important local fiesta. Gradings run from the 5-star luxury hotels, which conform to the highest international standards, to modest 1-star places styled as 'simple but comfortable', where you can get a double room for between £1.50 and £2.50 and three fixed-price meals for around £2.

Or maybe you prefer to stay in a castle?

Imagine watching the sunset from the battlements of a medieval fortress and taking a last stroll along the sentry-walk before going to bed . . . or living in a mansion once owned by a noble family, full of antique furniture, suits of armour and precious paintings . . . or sitting down to your evening meal in the refectory of a fifteenth-century convent, now softened with flowers and tapestries.

These three romantic places (the Virrey Toledo Castle at Oropesa, the Gil Blas mansion at Santillana del Mar and the former convent of San Francisco at Granada) are typical of more than fifty-three state-owned *Paradores Nacionales* which are strategically placed all over Spain. They are luxury hotels, most of them converted with great taste and skill from buildings of historic and architectural interest.

Admittedly, prices aren't cheap—rates rise sharply from around £2 for a double room—but it is really nothing for such style and elegance. And it is worth it just for one, unforgettable experience.

47

The Spanish Ministry of Tourism also operates a network of roadside *albergues*—modern inns catering mainly for motorists, often at remote spots where there is no alternative accommodation. Your stay is limited to forty-eight hours and rates range from about £2 to £4 for a double room. Some of the *albergues* have swimming pools and their restaurants feature local specialities. It's also worth knowing that you can get a snack at an *albergue* bar at any time.

A figure from the past

Returning late one night to my rickety old *pensión* in the labyrinth of streets behind Madrid's *Puerta del Sol*, I heard the tap-tapping of a stick on the pavement and the rattle of keys. Through the darkness, a strange figure appeared, in heavy cloak and hat, carrying a stave and wondrous assortment of keys on a huge ring.

It was the *sereno*, or night-watchman, who still has the powers of arrest, and is entrusted with the keys to all the doors in the street. Traditionally summoned by handclap, he will open your door, bid you a courteous goodnight and then vanish, tap-tapping into the distance.

Sadly, the *serenos* are slowly disappearing, and of those who remain, many wear what looks like a road-sweeper's cast-offs, with the addition of a peaked cap and truncheon. But their very existence conjures up memories of lampless streets, assassins, horse-drawn carriages with drawn blinds, romantic trysts and secret assignations; and for me, time always misses a heartbeat when I hear that tapping and rattling coming towards me through the darkened streets.

The possibility of bumping into the *sereno* is only one of the reasons why I prefer to stay at the ramshackle little *pensiónes* in the old quarter of most big Spanish cities.

The other is the price. You can get a double room for as little as 75p and a single for a couple of pence more, and that includes a washbasin with bracing cold water from the tap!

Pensiónes are also graded by the government from three to one star, and they provide acceptable standards at the lowest cost. The same grading covers *hosterias*. *Residencias* are hotels which do not provide meals other than breakfast.

When booking in at a *pensión*, you must make it clear from the start whether you want bed only, bed and breakfast or full pension terms, in which all meals are included in the bill. Some *pensiónes* (notably in Barcelona) will only accept guests on a full pension basis.

You'll find this the cheapest way of sleeping-and-eating but it can be a bit of a bore if you intend to stay out all day, or hope to sample local food at some of the cheap restaurants. Don't expect a rebate for meals not taken. If you accept full pension terms, you pay for the meal whether you've had it or not. How-

48

ever, most *pensiónes* are happy to settle for a bed and breakfast arrangement, which is also the accepted system in *residencias*.

Fallen stars

It is when the star rating stops and the authorities shrug their shoulders in despair that you discover Spain's rock-bottom accommodation . . . the *fondas* and *posadas*.

You share a room with two or three unshaven people you may never have seen before, eat in the kitchen, fetch your cold water from a tap in the stable (making sure not to walk behind the horses) and stumble about the dark for loos that would have appeared primitive in El Cid's time.

You can stay overnight for about 30p and meals are simple and equally cheap, usually consisting of soups, stews or potato-filled Spanish omelettes, with the type of local wine that would be better topping up a car battery.

Not long ago, I became a connoisseur of *posadas* when I travelled on horseback over the remote Las Alpujarras mountain range. Despite the frequently off-putting crudeness of the accommodation, I was always touched by the helpfulness of the innkeepers—including the man who, after I had been searching for the loo for an hour, replied patiently: '*Claro! Va con los caballos.*' (Obviously . . . you go with the horses.)

Posadas have never got around to accepting the twentieth century, and therefore do not advertise themselves. They have no signs, no notices, no identification. If you're tired, broke and in a small southern village (particularly between Malaga and Granada), just say: *Dígame, por favor; hay una posada aquí?* (Tell me, please; is there a posada here?) and you'll be directed to an inconspicuous door in the wall, behind which life hasn't changed for five hundred years.

Youth hostels

Spain's equivalent of our youth hostels are the *Albergues Juveniles*. There are about seventy of them, and the average cost of a bed is around 40 pesetas a night, with breakfast for 15 pesetas, lunch at 45 pesetas and supper 50 pesetas. Personally I still think *pensiónes* and *fondas* are better value, but the YHA, Trevelyan House, St Albans, Herts, will supply you with a list if you need it.

Carry on camping

Dog-tired and hungry, I pulled off the main road outside the Roman city of Merida not long ago, swerved past a notice saying *Prohibido el paso* and pitched camp under some pine trees. There were about twelve of us and we soon had a fire going and the stew sizzling. Three or four put up their tents, but the rest of us snuggled into our sleeping bags, pulled the groundsheets over us and went to sleep. Just after dawn, all hell broke loose. In an appalling din, we felt ourselves being trampled underfoot by what sounded like the entire Spanish infantry. Terrified, we peeped over our groundsheets . . . to discover that we were right in the middle of a sheep-herding route. Sticking blindly to their well-worn path, the flock of about two hundred had walked right over us.

Thank goodness there wasn't a policeman around, for I think we must have broken a record for infringing the law. Up before the magistrates, the charges would have read:

1 Pitching camp without permission of the landowner.
2 Ignoring a *Prohibido el paso* ('No admittance') sign.
3 Camping on land likely to be dangerous.
4 Camping unreasonably near the roadside.
5 Erecting more than three tents.
6 Exceeding the limit of ten people outside an official camping site.

As you can see, camping in the open in Spain can be fraught with difficulties. Apart from the rules mentioned, you must not camp on dry river beds, less than 150 metres from any source of drinking water, within any urban area or within one kilometre of an official site.

Although some of these rules are usually ignored (obviously it is virtually impossible to find a landowner to secure camping permission) it is still easier to stick to recognized sites. Apart from coastal areas, however, official sites are widely scattered and the standard is inconsistent, to put it mildly.

I remember staying at a beautiful site just outside Seville,

decorated with wrought iron grilles and huge pots of flowers, and the following night at a dreadful dump where I got a severe electric shock when I put a 5-peseta piece into the warm-shower machine. It turned out that previous users had converted it into a lethal weapon by feeding it with dud coins—which was rather hard on honest me!

Prices . . . and snags

A leaflet called *Mapa de campings*, showing all the official sites from Alva to Zaragoza, is available from the Spanish National Tourist Office in London. Sites are divided into 1st and 2nd Class and it is no longer necessary to possess a Camping Carnet, although this is still advisable for rough-camping as it includes third-party insurance.

Approximate daily rates at a 1st Class site are: adult 30–35 pesetas; child 20–25 pesetas; small tent, 25–30 pesetas; large tent 30–35 pesetas; car 30–35 pesetas; caravan or trailer 40–50 pesetas; motorcycles 20–25 pesetas; Dormobile 25–30 pesetas; coach 40–60 pesetas. On a 2nd Class site, rates drop to: adult, 25–30 pesetas; child 15–20 pesetas; small tent 15–25 pesetas; large tent 25–30 pesetas; car 25–30 pesetas; caravan 25–30 pesetas; motorcycles 15–20 pesetas; Dormobile 25–30 pesetas; coach 40–55 pesetas.

Unfortunately many camp sites are miles from the nearest town and way off any public transport routes, which means you are forced to spend the evening drinking morosely in the bar or cafeteria, and paying steeply for the privilege. The alternative is crouching like a tortoise in your darkened tent. Most camp sites have a supermarket, but prices are frequently extortionate, and it is much more sensible to stock up with food and oddments at the nearest village store.

All the same, I have a soft spot for the camp which featured on its menu 'Potatoes, camping style', translated into Spanish, German and French as *Patatas Camping*, *Kartoffeln Camping-Art* and *Pommes de terre Camping*. They turned out to be crisps.

EATING AND DRINKING

Telling the times

The package-tour holidaymakers had just arrived in Majorca and were enjoying their first meal in the hotel dining-room. All except one woman, who was getting more and more agitated. Finally, she got up and went over to the courier. 'It's the olive oil,' she said, quivering with indignation. 'You've got to do something about it, it's upsetting Albert.' She motioned to her husband, who was sitting glumly at the table.

Perplexed, as nobody had ever complained about olive oil before, the courier went to the manager. 'Olive oil?' the manager exploded. 'Now look, I learned about the British and olive oil fifteen years ago. I use peanut oil for cooking, I use lard, butter, but *never* a drop of olive oil!'

The courier crept back to the table, where the couple were still waiting grimly for satisfaction, and started to explain to them that they were mistaken about the olive oil in the food. The woman cut him short. 'We weren't complaining that they use it in the food,' she said. 'It's just that there is a cruet of it on the table and the very sight of it makes my Albert ill.'

It actually happened, and this obsession with olive oil and garlic is typical of the misconceptions many older people still have about Spanish food. The same determination to reduce Spain to 'England-with-sun' is responsible for the crowds of dejected British tourists you see sitting in restaurants at 7.30 in the evening, surrounded by a snowy sea of empty tables and pathetically trying to attract the attention of a non-existent waiter.

For the strangest thing about Spanish food is the times the Spanish eat it.

Like anywhere else, the day starts with breakfast or *Desayuno*, which in Spain rarely consists of anything heartier than a cup of coffee and a roll.

If you are staying with a family, or in a small rural inn, you might get *churros* or fried strips of batter, which the country people like to dip into large bowls of weak coffee.

This meagre breakfast results in a huge national hunger pang at around eleven in the morning, when many Spaniards take a break for a drink or sandwich, and bars, which a few minutes earlier had been deserted, suddenly fill with gesticulating customers.

Almuerzo, or lunch, is the biggest meal of the day, despite the heat, and isn't taken until around 3 o'clock in the afternoon, when it leads straight on to the siesta.

Most Spaniards resume work for a few hours before returning home to change for the traditional evening *paseo*, or stroll. This is why restaurants are empty until about 9 p.m. when they start to serve dinner, or *cena*.

Meal times tend to be earlier in the north and (mainly because of the insistent British clamour) in popular tourist hotels, but one of the delights of Spain is that you can always get some sort of meal at any time of the day in a café or bar.

Restaurants

You all know the sinking feeling when you enter a cheap-looking restaurant, only to find that it has been taken over by some crowd of local sophisticates and the prices are twice what you expected. You can't escape and you are committed to paying for a meal that will keep you on a starvation budget for a month.

It can't happen to you in Spain.

Menus and tariffs have to be prominently displayed outside by law and it is easy to compare prices before flexing your wallet and edging through the swing door. If you are on a tight budget, don't even bother to stop at restaurants whose windows are plastered with recommendations from touring associations and dining clubs; they are always on the expensive side.

In any town, there is a vast range of restaurants serving simple but satisfying meals for around 100 pesetas and it is more sensible to have a proper meal than rely on little snacks in bars, which are often surprisingly expensive (50 pesetas for a *ración* of fried mushrooms, for example).

Nearly all popular restaurants offer a *Menu Turístico*, which is a cheap, fixed-price meal giving you a choice of several items from the full menu, plus bread, wine or beer and a service charge. This used to be an admirable money-saving idea but the system is being increasingly abused by restaurants which limit you to a tiny selection of the cheapest dishes available—a fact you don't discover until you're safely inside. You also have to pay for a dish you might not want, like ice cream as the virtually compulsory sweet.

I find it more economic to order, say, soup and a main dish, with a half carafe of local wine, from the main menu.

Don't be put off by the appearance of the restaurant, or the suspicious look of some of the characters lounging inside. It's an odd feature of some small Spanish restaurants—notably the traditional *tascas* of Madrid—that the dining-room is hidden behind a scruffy and unprepossessing bar. Just ask for the *Comedor* and walk straight through.

In larger city cafeterias, watch out for two sets of prices, depending on whether you eat at the counter (*mostrador*) or sit at a table (*mesa*). As the difference can amount to several pesetas, wallet-watchers should jam themselves firmly against the counter and ignore all efforts to usher them to a table. The food will be exactly the same.

A lot to swallow

If you have a huge appetite, you'll find the biggest meals in the fertile north of Spain, with fish featuring strongly on the menu. In central Castile, the great speciality is *cochinillo asado* and *cordero asado*—roast sucking pig and baby lamb—but they are both rather expensive. Andalucian *gazpacho* is a delicious iced soup, throbbing with garlic and sprinkled with cucumber, green pepper, tomato, onion and breadcrumbs. Along the southern coast, the famous dish is *paella*, a savoury mixture of saffron rice packed with chicken, peppers and shellfish and served boiling hot in an iron dish. Chicken is excellent in Spain, bearing no resemblance to the tasteless polystyrene imitation you often get in Britain, and fish can be eaten safely far inland, thanks to the refrigerated trains and lorries which rush seafood from the coast each day. Pork (*cerdo*) and veal (*ternero*) feature on every menu, but whatever you do avoid steak—unless you have jaws like a waste-disposal unit and a stomach like a G.P.O. mailbag.

Spanish food is seldom served piping hot. They say it spoils the flavour and, anyway, the sun will provide all the heat you need. And in small country places, it is still a tradition to use only one knife and fork for everything. As soon as each empty plate is whipped away, you wipe the cutlery on your napkin and use it again. So don't let it go.

Just a snack

Compulsive snack-nibblers, the Spanish munch their way through an extraordinary variety of titbits during the day. If you see what look like fried onion-rings on a cafeteria counter, they are probably *calamares*, or squid, and taste much better than they sound. An even more bizarre item is *criadillas*, or sheep's testicles, which taste very much like sweetbreads. For years, I was completely perplexed by the most grotesque dish of them all. They look like amputated human fingers and were labelled *percebes*. Eventually it was explained that they were what we would call 'goose barnacles'. You strip off a gaiter-like covering and the flesh underneath is said to be succulent. I took their word for it.

These smaller dishes often accompany drinks in bars and the day's selection is usually scrawled on a blackboard above the counter.

But it is possible to get *free* food with your drinks. These are the traditional *tapas*—little dishes containing a sardine, a portion of cheese, crisps, nuts, olives or pieces of salt pork—which are included in the price of the drink. So with a little judicious ordering, you can eat for nothing.

Unlike British pubs, you can order coffee or soft drinks at Spanish bars and cafés and there are no restrictions on age; indeed, they are regarded far more as a family meeting place.

Alcohol is extremely cheap, and you can easily find yourself paying more for the Cola than the rum in a *cuba libre*. The Spaniards themselves stick to beer (*cerveza*), wine, sherry, brandy and the colourless but potent *anis*. Local gin (*ginebra*) is growing in popularity—most of the popular brands have highly unconvincing English-sounding names—but under no circumstances order Scotch. It is imported from Britain and will hit your money-belt where it hurts most.

The Spanish for sherry is *Jerez* (pronounced 'hereth') and it is the name of the prosperous town in Andalucia where most of the wine comes from. It is not drunk with meals but as an apéritif, often chilled. *Fino* is a pale and dry variety, *amontillado* is slightly sweeter but still on the dry side and *oloroso* is near what we would call a 'cream sherry'. Sherry is fortified with brandy and is therefore much stronger than it appears. You may put it into a trifle, but it isn't to be trifled with.

During meals, the best thing to drink is local carafe wine, which is cheaper and less heady than the branded varieties. Ask for *vino de casa* or *vino corriente*, either *tinto* (red) or *blanco* (white). Spanish champagne is wet, cheap and fizzy and that is just about all that can be said for it, but an excellent refresher in hot weather is *sangría*, a sparkling mixture of red wine, lemonade, fruit and liqueurs, served ice cold in a large jug.

You can't take it with you

Search as hard as you like, there's one popular Spanish drink you'll never find outside Spain. It is called *horchata* and, every year, Spaniards quaff nearly 20 million pints of the soft, milky liquid. But it's no use a tourist getting a taste for it, for *horchata* doesn't keep longer than forty-eight hours. It is extracted from an edible, potato-like plant called *chufa*. This is washed, cut and crushed, and water and sugar are then mixed with the paste. A pound of *chufas* can produce about two pints of *horchata* and the centre of the industry is the town of La Huerta, near Valencia, in which more than 5 million *chufas* are gathered each year . . . almost enough to fulfil the entire demand for the drink.

Drinking for free

One of Spain's best-kept secrets is that you can enjoy some of her finest drinks absolutely free.

At Jerez de la Frontera, you can visit the famous sherry bodegas, follow the entire manufacturing process and sample *finos, amontillados* and *olorosos.* All you have to do is pick whatever bodega takes your fancy—they are all conspicuously signposted—wait in the foyer until one of the conducted parties assembles and then tag on the end.

It is the same happy story at San Sadurni, near Barcelona, where most of the champagne is produced. The caves are open to visitors throughout the season—Cordoniu is highly recommended—and you can trace the fascinating development of the wine, with plenty of 'educational aids'.

My last memory of San Sadurni was of a couple of jovial young Irishmen in white shirts and grey flannels who slid into our party and proceeded to drink the free glasses at an alarming rate, almost as if they might never taste the stuff again. Eventually, I asked them where they were spending their holiday. They weren't. They were theological students training for the priesthood at a nearby seminary and it was their afternoon off.

Looking for the loo

All this talk about eating and drinking is a natural introduction to the subject of 'Spanish tummy'. Most British tourists go down with this complaint sooner or later and immediately blame the water, the food, the drains, the olive oil, the heat, but never themselves. In my experience, Spanish tummy is caused by one, or a combination, of the following things: the local water, over-indulgence in cheap alcohol, drinking cold drinks in hot sun (on the beach, for example) and, more than anything, the ice. Like cigarettes in Britain, every chunk of Spanish ice should carry a government health warning. People who wouldn't even dream of cleaning their teeth in Spanish tap water gaily swallow pounds of the ghastly stuff in their drinks every day. If only they could see it delivered to the back door of the bar early in the morning, wrapped in dirty sacking and followed by a retinue of flies. My foolproof antidote against Spanish tummy consists of two words, *Sin hielo*—without ice.

Which brings me, inevitably, to loos.

As some kind of revenge for the indignities imposed on her by mass tourism, it is almost impossible to find a public lavatory in Spain, even if you could work out the correct word to use.

In fact there are very few public conveniences even in the big cities, and in most small towns none at all. If you do want a loo, you must march bravely into a café or bar and ask to use theirs. It is the accepted thing, so there is no need to be embarrassed.

The problem is: What is it called?

At various times, it has been *El retrete, Caballeros y Señoras, La Tocado* (for women, the word being the equivalent of 'powder room'), WC (pronounced 'uwee ethay'), Le Water (pronounced 'vater'), the dreadfully named *El urinario* and, the latest, *Los Servicios*.

Stick to *Los Servicios* and you can't wander too far off the mark. When you get there, *Caballeros* is the men's and *Señoras* the women's. Sometimes they are labelled 'WC' and 'WS (*Water Caballeros* and *Water Señoras*, believe it or not) and in really *cursi* (or pretentious) places, the men's is indicated by a wrought-iron pipe and the women's by a fan. And if you are wondering what to do when faced (as you probably will be) by a hole in the ground and two footplates, the solution is simple. You squat.

Take a tip

At least tipping in Spain is easy. Nearly all bills automatically include a service charge of between 10 per cent and 15 per cent, and there is no need whatsoever to tip any further. It is customary, however, to leave a few pesetas extra by overpaying your bill to the nearest round figure. For example, if your bill for a few drinks or a meal is 98 pesetas, leave the change from a 100-peseta note on the saucer. Never overtip. It embarrasses the Spaniard and creates an unfortunate precedent for others. The Germans have a saying, 'To tip like a Spaniard.' Which means hardly at all.

7 Making the most of it

Don't just sit there, do something

My favourite guide-book doesn't mince its words. 'In Spain', it
warns, 'lock your bedroom door and make sure there isn't room
for a man to hide behind pictures and furniture, for robbery and
murder go hand in hand.'

Actually, these hints for the unwary traveller appear in
Philip Thicknesse's *Continental Travels*, published in 1770, but
judging by the unadventurous way some tourists carry on in
Spain, they could still be true.

I once went on a cheap trip to Majorca with two hundred
British holidaymakers, of whom half never ventured from the
hotel. During the day they sat round the pool ordering drinks,
and at night a ghostly hush descended on the hotel while they all
bent their heads to Bingo.

The whole thing struck me as a sad misuse of the wonderful
opportunities that cheap, package holidays can bring. To me,
the whole point of going on a low-cost, all-inclusive trip is to use
it as a beginning, not an end.

With your return flight, accommodation and breakfast all
paid for, you can afford to skip the other meals and use your
hotel as a base from which to explore the countryside. If funds
are low—or you can't travel more than 500 yards without
hunger pangs—your hotel will always provide a packed lunch
provided you order it the night before.

Of course, some places are better situated than others. Any
package resort in Majorca is good as a springboard for expeditions, and on the Costa Brava you are within easy reach of the
ancient walled town of Pals, the pottery centre of La Bisbal,
Besalu with its Roman bridge, the ruined Graeco-Roman city
of Ampurias and Gerona, where the cathedral possesses a
fourteenth-century silver altar. On the other hand, Benidorm,
backed by uninteresting hinterland, is a poor choice.

My unlikely favourite is Torremolinos, a welter of concrete
and neon, yet perfectly placed for exploring the whole of
Andalucia. The resounding cities of Granada, Ronda, Malaga
and Cordoba can all be covered on a day trip, and a little extra
map-reading will reveal gems like the twelfth-century fortified
village of Castellar, Ojen, a fiercely whitewashed mountain
hamlet with one road in and no road out, and the Cave of
Piletas, where prehistoric man has left strange scratches on the
walls which experts believe could represent the first attempt at a
written language.

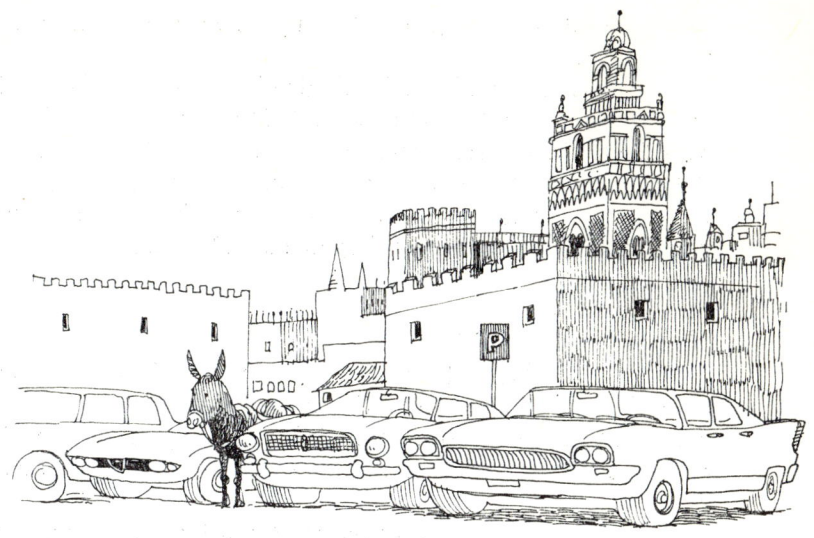

The secret of getting the most out of Spain is to do yous homework in advance. You can get excellent large-scale mapt of Spain (Firestone and Michelin are the best) from specialisr firms like Edward Stanford Ltd, London, and the Spanish National Tourist Office publishes detailed region-by-region guides.

Provided you hold a valid driving licence, there are no problems in hiring a car once you arrive, though you should make sure you get an international driving licence from the AA or RAC before you go, as Spain is one of the few countries that still insist on them. It is an impressive-looking grey booklet in several languages, complete with passport photograph, and it will cost you £1.

Car hire rates vary from company to company but it is false economy to choose the cheapest. Many small *Coches para Alquiler* firms give their vehicles the most perfunctory servicing —I have often taken delivery of a car stuffed to the air-vents with rubbish left behind by the previous user—and it is wise to stick to the larger more reputable firms, like the government-controlled *ATESA*.

Roughly, a small Seat 600 (the Spanish-made version of a Fiat, which a racing-driver friend of mine refers to as a 'motorized pram') costs 300 pesetas a day, plus 3 pesetas for each kilometre covered.

There is usually a 2,000-pesetas deposit (refunded when you return the car) and it is important to check whether the price includes full insurance. Personal accident and medical cover can be taken out in Britain and £2 or so is a small price to pay for peace of mind—as I discovered when a homicidal Spanish driver, hurtling towards me on the wrong side of the road,

59

forced me into an olive grove at 60 mph. I've never been keen on olives since.

Scooters and mopeds can be hired at lower rates, mainly in the popular resorts, and on the island of Minorca I once ended up with the most extraordinary vehicle since the Gentlewomen's Velocipede. It was a car whose body was made entirely of wickerwork, with a wicker roof surrounded by a scarlet, tasselled fringe. It was like riding in a laundry basket.

All the fun of the fiasco

Judging by the leaflet thrust into my hand, the fiesta was going to be the biggest thing to hit Spain since the Reconquest. Even taking into account conventional Spanish hyperbole, the ultimate in drama and excitement was clearly about to be unleashed upon us.

'Grand Regatta and procession across the bay of magnificently decorated boats. . . . Thrilling boat race with a superb prize for the winner. . . . Great tug-of-war between adults and children. . . . Stupendous display of fireworks. . . . Extraordinary cavalcade of vintage vehicles with passengers in period costume. . . . Wonderful launching of balloons with prizes. . . . Great and spectacular final carnival with election of Beauty Queen.'

That was before the chaos set in.

From the word go, there appeared to be no co-operation at all between the organizers of the various events, who treated each other with the deepest suspicion.

The first the local Mayor heard of the cavalcade of vintage cars—borrowed from the collection of a wealthy American living near by—was when he read it in the handbill. Miffed at not being consulted, he banned the parade, commenting, 'If those cars come in here, I'll punch the leader on the nose!'

A compromise was reached by allowing a few of the cars to drive quickly in and out of the village on another day. The result was that odd people in period costume were left roaming the streets on the advertised day, trying vainly to find the procession. One eccentric came down from the hills in a decorated horse-cart, with his brother dressed as a woman and twirling a parasol. They returned, highly disgruntled, with the jeers of the crowd ringing in their ears.

The Grand Regatta consisted of five fishing smacks furtively sneaking across the harbour and only four rowing-boats competed in the 'Thrilling boat race'. One failed to start, the second sprang a leak half way, the third lost its oars and the winner's 'superb prize' turned out to be an outsize *ensaimada*, or bun.

The children who lost the tug-of-war burst into tears and when a local café owner promised to pacify all the losers with free lemonade, he found that the team had mysteriously multiplied by the time it reached his shop.

60   Something went wrong with the gas cylinders and the balloons

shot into the air, never to be seen again. The first fireworks failed to go off, and when they were replaced by highly explosive fog maroons, the crowd scattered in terror. As if all this wasn't enough, the beauty queen's crown was won by a French girl, the daughter of a visitor, who was booed by the locals.

The whole affair was a complete fiasco and everyone had a wonderful time. As a cameo of parochial Spanish life it was priceless, and yet it happened in a fishing village only a few miles from the most tourist-crammed area of Majorca.

Fiestas come in many forms in Spain, though most have a religious origin, commemorating a local patron saint, a holy festival or a popular place of pilgrimage or worship. Not that the Church lays a sombre hand on the merrymaking. In its sheer fun and exuberance, the Spanish fiesta is a reminder that the word holiday is only a corruption of 'holy day'.

Fiestas offer a welcome break from work, notably in rural areas, and the calendar is full of *romerías* (festive processions, usually to a local shrine), *verbenas* (evening celebrations with music and dancing), *ferias* (great fairs, frequently lasting for days), and *fallas* (processions of giant papier-mâché figures, often satirical, which are burned on the last night).

Some fiestas are world-famous, like the deeply moving celebration of Easter Week in Seville, followed by a fortnight of processions, bullfights and carnival, and the Fiesta of St Fermín in Pamplona, where the bulls chase the crowds through the streets in the *encierro*.

But a glance at the Spanish Tourist Office's 'Calendar of Festivals' (the eight regional booklets are available free) reveals a wealth of small, local red-letter days which are just as much fun, and less likely to be swamped by tourists. You may even come across a really good fiasco.

You are Here

If you are a stranger in town, one word can solve most of your problems: *Turismo*. Follow this signpost and you can't go far wrong. It will lead you to the local office of the *Ministerio de Información y Turismo*, where you can get advice on accommodation, car hire, places of interest, entertainments and routes. Stuff your duffle-bag with all the brochures and leaflets you can find, for they are full of useful information about the area and surrounding districts. It is a lot easier to pick up brochures on the way, and then junk them, than carry a whole library of literature with you from home.

Most *Turismo* offices also hand out town-plans, though the best all-round selection is in the annual and invaluable Michelin Guide to Spain (£1.20), which includes sightseeing information and lists of hotels and restaurants, from the most luxurious to the medium-modest.

Where there is no *Turismo* office, a quick way of deciding whether a village possesses any worthwhile sights is to go into the tobacconist's shop and look at the picture postcards. If there's anything even remotely interesting in the area, some enterprising local photographer will have snapped it and churned out a handful of pictures.

Unlike many village shops, tobacconists are easy to find. At first glance, they all look as though they are run by the most patriotic man in town. They are decorated in red and gold, the Spanish national colours, or bear a conspicuous red-and-gold sign with the words *Tabacalera Expendeduria S.A.* Known as the *Estanco*, it is the place where you buy not only tobacco, cigarettes and other bits and pieces, but also postage stamps (*sellos*).

A postcard back to Britain needs a 5-peseta stamp (*Un sello de cinco pesetas*), and a letter 8 pesetas (*Un sello de ocho pesetas*). While you're licking your *sellos*, look around for one of those old-fashioned 'Shepherds' cigarette lighters' with a thick, yard-long orange wick. They only cost a few pesetas and even if you don't need to light your ciggy in a howling gale, the wick has a hundred uses, from securing your suitcase to holding up your trousers.

Pillar-boxes in town are generally painted silver with a red-and-gold stripe, but in villages you'll have to keep your eyes skinned for an inconspicuous, weatherbeaten slit in a wall bearing the word *Correos*.

What's in store?

Unlike the *estanco*, other shops aren't so easy to locate, particularly in southern rural *pueblos*. I spent a whole morning in Jeres de Marquesada, a fiercely whitewashed Andalucian mountain village with balconies brimming with flowers, searching for a single shop. Surely the whole place hasn't reverted to barter? I wondered. The explanation was simple. There were shops, but they were only small, windowless rooms. 'In the strong sunlight, anything we put in a window would be ruined in a few days,' a shopkeeper told me. 'So we do without windows.' The clue is to look for a bead or chain curtain where a door should be. On the other side is your shop.

Naturally, all towns have shopping centres like ours, with department stores and self-service *supermercados*. If you are stocking-up on food, remember that words like *rebaja, oferta* and *oportunidad* on the supermarket shelves are the Spanish equivalent of our '2p Off'. I always head straight for the *mercado central*, the covered market where Spanish housewives crowd round stalls piled high with fresh fruit and vegetables. Bigger markets also sell meat, fish, cheese, eggs and groceries— all cheaper than you'll find in the high-street shops. Most *mercados centrales* start as early as 7 a.m. and finish at lunchtime, so it is important to grab your shopping-basket and arrive promptly for the best selection, even if you can't stop yawning.

Just like anywhere else, there are good and bad buys in Spain. Don't waste your pesetas on toilet preparations, cosmetics, general clothing, camera film, confectionery and cheapjack souvenirs. All these things are cheaper or better in Britain and you should take all you need with you. Conversely, you'll get superior value if you buy embroidery (particularly handkerchiefs), leatherware, cutlery (I have a spectacular set of damascened Toledo cutlery in black and gold which cost me £12 for 18 pieces and makes my dinner guests think I'm a millionaire), women's shoes, pottery, tiles, glass, olivewood tableware, bygones (like eighteenth-century iron door locks, huge keys and apothecaries' jars), glass lampshades, woven cushion covers, rugs and even colourfully decorated donkey harness.

Wherever you go in Spain, you will come across strange figures, often blind or lame, carrying banner-like poles covered with fluttering scraps of paper, or with pieces pinned and flapping against their chests. Like souls in torment, they roam the streets crying in a melancholy tone, *Que bonito numero para hoy!* ('A lucky number for you today!') or just *Para hoy!* They are the ticket-sellers for the state lottery, a job generally reserved for handicapped people. Tickets are expensive, anything up to 5,000 pesetas, but most people only buy a portion or join a syndicate to invest in a larger share. Sometimes, an entire village wins a prize, maybe *El Gordo* 'The Fat One', or jackpot. If you fancy a flutter, tip the seller a couple of pesetas. It is considered good luck.

Sole brothers

A brush with a *limpiabotas* isn't so lucky. *Limpiabotas*, or shoeshine boys, are the predators of the streets, forever on the prowl

with their battered footstools containing polishes and cleaning gear. The slightest hesitation while you're sitting at a café table and they will descend on your feet with wildly flapping dusters and flying brushes. As the *limpiabotas* often make no distinction between leather shoes, suèdes and open-toe sandals, the result can be expensive. They sometimes carry a secret supply of stick-on rubber soles which they slap onto your shoes without warning and then—because they cannot be removed—ask an outrageous price. Author Ernest Hemingway, who as an inveterate café lounger was sitting prey for the *limpiabotas*, swore that the only way to keep them at bay was to walk around barefoot. Even then, I suspect, they would try to fix rubber soles to your feet. The only way to deal with *limpiabotas* is a repeated *Gracias, no!* keeping your feet firmly under the table.

The Spanish themselves have a sympathetic attachment to *limpiabotas* which stems from the days when *caballeros*, or gentlemen, travelled by horse while *peones*, or peasants, plodded through the muddy streets on foot. Consequently, you could always tell a *caballero* by his shiny shoes. Even now, Spanish men are meticulous about clean shoes and, while the *limpiabotas* can still juggle their brushes, the tradition will never die out.

Let sleeping dogbeaters lie

The oldest part of any Spanish city usually centres round the Cathedral and sooner or later you will feel the urge to slip through those huge, creaking doors and see for yourself these great treasure-houses of a deep and abiding faith. So beware of the dogbeater, or *Azotaperros*.

The job of the *Azotaperros*, officially known as the *Silencarios*, is to prevent anyone entering who is improperly dressed.

During the tourist season, the *Silencarios* are kept on their toes, barring the way to girls in hotpants, bikini tops or bare shoulders, men in shorts or bare chests and anyone puffing a cigarette. Religious custom in Spain dictates that girls should have their heads and bare arms covered when entering a holy building and scarves are usually available at the door in case you forget. To observe these simple rules is merely a matter of respect, and to flout them demonstrates nothing but bad manners. I have seen some atrocious behaviour by tourists in Spanish churches, some of the worst offenders being groups of young French Catholics. In Teguise, a tiny township on the Canary Island of Lanzarote, the convent church of Santa Domingo was actually closed to visitors after repeated desecration by tourists. Coach parties would arrive drunk after enjoying a wine-tasting near by and roam around the church scratching their names on the walls, chipping off pieces of plaster or wood as souvenirs and even climbing on the altar to get a closer look at the Virgin. You now have to make a special appointment with the caretaker to get the key.

The *Azotaperros* may no longer chase out dogs, but he is still a useful man to have around.

An eye for the girls

Not long ago, Spanish beaches had their version of the *Azotaperros*, usually a couple of uniformed wardens nicknamed 'The Navel Patrol' who kept a lookout for girls in skimpy bikinis. It was considered a most sought-after job but, with the gradual relaxation of rules governing beachwear in Spain, the patrollers have nearly all been pensioned off. You can now wear the briefest costume without any fear of a shawl being thrown over you and outraged citizens bundling you off to the police station.

A death blow was dealt to the Peeping Patrol years ago when the film actress Brigitte Bardot, told that her two-piece swimsuit was not allowed, replied, 'All right, which part do you want me to take off?'

Understandably, people still take offence if you wander off the beach into the streets without covering up with a bathrobe or shirt-and-trousers. I felt very sorry for one English girl I saw who tripped from a hotel swimming-pool into the street in Palma, Majorca, blissfully unaware that all the whispers of the passers-by were not compliments on her bikini-uncovered figure but mutters of *Sin verguenza!*, or 'Shameful!'

In step with the times

Shop hours in Spain can be eccentric and if you stick to British ideas you'll return empty-handed with the word *Cerrado* dancing before your eyes. It is a word familiar to thousands of frustrated British tourists, and means 'Closed'. To make sure the shops are *Abierto*—the reverse side of the sign, meaning 'Open'—remember that trading times in Spain are often dictated by the weather. When the sun is at its height, the Spanish take their afternoon siesta and many southern towns have a ghostly, deserted look as though the entire population has fled. Sensibly, the shopkeepers pull down their shutters too.

Shops also turn their signs to *Cerrado* on Sundays, fiesta days and public holidays. Generally, shops are open from 9 a.m. until 1.30 p.m. and reopen from 4.30 p.m. until 7.30 p.m. or later. When the pesetas start running dry and you want to cash your travellers' cheques, you have to be nippy on your feet to catch the banks with their *Abierto* showing. Business hours are usually 9 a.m. until 1 p.m. in summer, except on Saturday when they close at 12 noon, and from 9 a.m. until 4 p.m. in winter (Saturdays 12.30 p.m.). These times can vary from region to region, but if you are caught without money, many travel agents, nearly all hotel reception desks and occasional foreign-exchange counters (look for the sign *Cambio*) change travellers' cheques and banknotes. Big stores will sometimes accept travellers' cheques for reasonably large purchases. In each case you must produce your passport.

Just the job

The cheapest way of going on holiday is to get paid for it. Far from battering your bank balance, you could return from Spain with a few pesetas profit jingling in your pocket.

The A.N.U.E.* arranges work camps during the summer and although most of the effort is voluntary, some camps pay pocket money. Free maintenance is also provided on the archaeological and social schemes organized for young people between sixteen and twenty-five by the Delegacion Nacional de Juventud.

For a deeper insight into the country, vacation courses will introduce you to other young people and accommodation is frequently with families. You can study art, language, history, religion, literature, even take a secretarial course in Spanish, and excursions are sometimes included in the programme. One course which would have me packing my toothbrush and tuning-fork before you could say Ole! is 'Flamenco Study and Instruction', held in a beautiful Andalucian country house, the *Finca Espartero*, at Moron de la Frontera, near Seville. Details of a comprehensive range of holiday-study programmes are available from the Central Bureau for Educational Visits and Exchanges and the Instituto de Espana in London. The Bureau also publishes helpful booklets on cheap student travel, school trips to Spain and student exchanges.

* Full addresses of all organizations mentioned are given on page 69.

Not all package-tours dump you on a beach, stuff you with three meals a day and fly you back when you're brown and broke. Some specialist firms offer unusual and worthwhile holidays which it would be almost impossible (or prohibitively expensive) to organize on your own. R.A.S. Holidays will take you dinghy sailing on the Costa Brava, mountaineering in the Picos de Europa or walking across Majorca. You can go on a painting trip to Palamos or Castro Urdiales with Galleon World Travel, and Aventura makes the most thrilling journey of them all, a horseback expedition across the Sierra Nevada mountains.

The easiest way to get an intimate and human view of Spanish life—without even leaving your armchair—is by corresponding with a Spanish penfriend. Addresses and introductions are available from the International Friendship League, International Scholastic Correspondence and the Educational Institute of Scotland (see page 70).

Getting the right answer

There's one big snag about repeating sentences from a phrase book. It doesn't tell you what to do when, prompted by your apparent fluency, a native replies in a voluble stream of French, German or Italian. Stunned by the response to their carefully enunciated questions, many tourists end up asking plaintively, 'What does he say?'. Which brings you right back to where you started.

For years a friend of mine thought *No funciona* ('Out of order') was the Spanish for Lift, so it is obviously essential to know *some* basic Spanish phrases. More important is the goodwill they create. Resigned to so many English-only tourists whose idea of communication is, 'If they can't understand, say it louder', the Spanish are delighted beyond measure if someone actually takes the trouble to learn a few words of their language. The response is out of proportion to the effort involved.

Although basic Spanish is quite easy, certain words and phrases can catch you unawares. If you feel shy or bashful when a Spaniard asks you to dance, don't use the word *embarazada* or you really will be embarrassed. It means pregnant. *Constipado* is the odd Spanish word for a cold and although *Estoy* means 'I am' and *Caliente* is 'hot', never say *estoy caliente*, however sweltering the weather. The Spanish use a similar construction to the French, *Tengo calor* ('I have heat').

Mañana is another slippery word. It means 'morning' but also 'tomorrow', so 'tomorrow morning' becomes *Mañana por la mañana* in the same way that 'tomorrow night' is *Mañana por la noche*.

Having dodged the problem of *mañana*, you're now faced with the question, 'When is an afternoon not an afternoon?' The Spanish for 'Good afternoon' is *Buenas tardes,* a phrase you'll hear late in the evening, right until the moment *Buenas noches* ('Good night') takes over. Theoretically, 'Good night' should be used from dusk onwards, and don't be offended if a Spanish friend comes up to you, shakes hands and says *Buenas noches*. It is used equally as a greeting.

Dear sir or madam

Meeting people is where your troubles really start. To Britons, used to simple Jack Smiths and Betty Joneses, Spanish names are incredibly complicated and you can easily upset a Spaniard by inadvertently turning him into a woman.

This alarming possibility stems from the Spanish habit of adding their mother's name to their own. A glance at any Spanish business-man's visiting card usually reveals a double-barrelled name, say José Manuel López Arriaga (or López y Arriaga). The temptation would be to call him Senor Arriaga, which would be wrong. Arriaga is his mother's maiden name and he would be referred to as Senor López.

The custom occasionally causes confusion when the Spanish apply it to British surnames. If your name is George Robinson and you've been waiting for days for a letter which should have arrived, try peeping in the hotel pigeon-hole marked 'G' in case the Spanish clerk has filed it under what he assumed was your correct surname.

The Spanish are a polite people and employ many courtesy phrases in their everyday conversation. When you say *gracias* ('thank you') in a shop after making a purchase, the assistant will often reply, *de nada* ('Don't mention it'). Sometimes, it is pleasant to be able to return the compliment by observing a social nicety oneself. On train journeys, it is customary for complete strangers to unwrap their sausages or sandwiches and offer them round. You neither scoff the lot nor mutter a curt *No, gracias*, but decline the offer with a polite *Buen provecho*.

A final look back

So we come to the end of our journey. We have seen many things and absorbed many impressions and I only hope I have succeeded in communicating to you some of my love of Spain. In the end, the essential character of a country depends on its people, and centuries of conflict and toil have endowed the Spanish with a quality of indomitability which is one of their deepest virtues. To me, this quality achieves an almost symbolic character. Wherever you go in Spain, be it some harsh and lonely landscape from which even the birds have fled from the metallic sun, you will see in the distance a lone human figure. It is always there, as if deliberately placed by God as a sign of reassurance to the traveller. In the end, Spain's proudest possession is the Spanish.

Appendix: Useful addresses

General
SPANISH NATIONAL TOURIST OFFICE, 70 Jermyn Street, London SW1 (Tel. 01-930-8578). Vast range of free maps, guides, brochures and lists. Information service.

EDWARD STANFORD LTD, 12 Long Acre, London WC2 (Tel. 01-836-7863). Specialists in guide-books and maps.

CENTRAL BUREAU FOR EDUCATIONAL VISITS AND EXCHANGES, 43 Dorset Street, London W1H 3FN (Tel. 01-486-5101). Booklets (35p post free) include Working Holidays Abroad, Vacation Courses Abroad, Youth and Student Travel, School Travel and Exchange.

Student travel and accommodation
NATIONAL UNION OF STUDENTS, Comisaria para el SEU, Glorieta de Quevedo 8, Madrid 10, Spain.

NATIONAL STUDENT TRAVEL OFFICE, Oficina de Viajes de la Comiseria para el SEU (Viajesu), Fernando el Catolico 88, Madrid 16.

NUS TRAVEL, 117 Euston Road, London NW1 25X.

RED ESPANOLA DE ALBERGUES JUVENILES, Jose Ortega y Gasset 71, Madrid 6. List of youth hostels.

Finding a job
VACATION-WORK, 9 Park End Street, Oxford OX1 1RJ. Publishes *The Directory of Summer Jobs Abroad* (90p).

Working holidays
A.N.U.E., Marques de Erquijo 11, Madrid 8. Details of voluntary work-camps.

CHRISTIAN MOVEMENT FOR PEACE, Stowford House, Bayswater Road, Oxford (Mrs L. Green). Sends volunteers to international work camps in Spain. You work around six hours a day, with free board and accommodation.

Vacation courses
INSTITUTO DE ESPANA, 102 Eaton Square, London SW1W 9AN (Tel. 01-235-1484/5). Lists of study courses in Spain.

BRITISH INSTITUTE, Calle Almagro 5, Madrid 4. Information on study courses.

CENTRO CULTURAL HISPANICO, Doctor Castelo 32, Madrid 9.

Specialist holidays

R.A.S. HOLIDAYS LTD., Wings House, Bridge Road East, Welwyn Garden City, Herts. (Tel. Welwyn Garden 31133 and 91-435-7181). Climbing, walking, sailing holidays in Spain and the Balearics.

GALLEON WORLD TRAVEL ASSOCIATION LTD, 45 Cathedral Place, London EC4M 7PB (Tel. 01-236-2636, Glasgow 041-332-3521/2, Manchester 061-834-8315/6, Bristol 28392/28721, Birmingham 021-236-6414/5). Painting tours to Palamos, Cadaques and Castro Urdiales.

AVENTURA, 10 Broad Street, Hereford HR4 9AG (Tel. 0432-55311), and 122 Knightsbridge, London SW1X 7PG (Tel. 589-0016). Expeditions on horseback through the Sierra Nevada range in parties of eight. Some riding experience essential.

ATESA, 35 Piccadilly, London W1V 9PB (Tel. 01-734-7282). Specialized coach tours of Spain, including art cities and 'Castles in Spain'. Also car-hire in advance.

SOUTHERN FERRIES, Arundel Towers, Portland Terrace, Southampton SO9 4AE. Car and passenger ferries Southampton-Algeciras and San Sebastian (Pasajes de San Juan).

SWEDISH LLOYD LTD, Lloyd House, Baker Street, London W1M 1LA. Car and passenger ferries Southampton-Bilbao. Also 'mini-cruises' to northern Spain.

Penfriends

INTERNATIONAL FRIENDSHIP LEAGUE, Penfriend Service, 16 Beaulieu Road, North End, Portsmouth PO2 0DN. All ages.

INTERNATIONAL SCHOLASTIC CORRESPONDENCE, "Dovenden", Tipton St John, Sidmouth, Devon EX10 0AH. Ages 11-16.

THE EDUCATIONAL INSTITUTE OF SCOTLAND, 46 Moray Place, Edinburgh EH3 63H. Ages 8-18.

Index